Estimated Loads of Suspended Sediment and Selected Trace Elements Transported Through the Clark Fork Basin, Montana, in Selected Periods Before and After the Breach of Milltown Dam (Water Years 1985–2009)

By Steven K. Sando and John H. Lambing

In cooperation with the U.S. Environmental Protection Agency

Scientific Investigations Report 2011–5030

U.S. Department of the Interior
U.S. Geological Survey

U.S. Department of the Interior
KEN SALAZAR, Secretary

U.S. Geological Survey
Marcia K. McNutt, Director

U.S. Geological Survey, Reston, Virginia: 2011

For more information on the USGS—the Federal source for science about the Earth, its natural and living resources, natural hazards, and the environment, visit http://www.usgs.gov or call 1-888-ASK-USGS

For an overview of USGS information products, including maps, imagery, and publications, visit http://www.usgs.gov/pubprod

To order this and other USGS information products, visit http://store.usgs.gov

Suggested citation:
Sando, S.K., and Lambing, J.H., 2011, Estimated loads of suspended sediment and selected trace elements transported through the Clark Fork basin, Montana, in selected periods before and after the breach of Milltown Dam (water years 1985–2009): U.S. Geological Survey Scientific Investigations Report 2011–5030, 64 p.

Contents

Figures

Tables

Conversion Factors, Datum, Abbreviated Units, and Acronyms

Multiply	By	To obtain
acre	0.4047	hectare (ha)
acre-foot (acre-ft)	1,233	cubic meter (m³)
cubic yard (yd³)	0.7647	cubic meter (m³)
cubic foot per second (ft³/s)	0.02832	cubic meter per second (m³/s)
foot (ft)	0.3048	meter (m)
gallon (gal)	3.785	liter (L)
mile (mi)	1.609	kilometer (km)
ounce (oz)	28,350	milligram (mg)
ounce (oz)	28,350,000	microgram (µg)
pound, avoirdupois (lb)	0.4536	kilogram (kg)
square mile (mi²)	2.590	square kilometer (km²)
ton, short (2,000 lb)	0.9072	megagram (Mg)
ton per day	0.9072	metric ton per day
ton per year	0.9072	metric ton per year

Horizontal coordinate information is referenced to the North American Datum of 1927 (NAD 27).

Water year is the 12-month period from October 1 through September 30 of the following calendar year. The water year is designated by the calendar year in which it ends. For example, water year 2009 is the period from October 1, 2008, through September 30, 2009.

Abbreviated units and symbol used in this report:

acre-ft	acre-feet
ft	feet
ft³/s	cubic feet per second
µg/L	micrograms per liter
µg/g	micrograms per gram
mg/L	milligrams per liter
mi	miles
mi²	square miles
mm	millimeter
µm	micrometer
yd³	cubic yards
<	less than

Acronyms used in this report:

AMLE	adjusted maximum likelihood estimation
ASQ	arsenic discharge
CDQ	cadmium discharge
CUQ	copper discharge
FEQ	iron discharge
LOG	logarithm (base 10)
LOWESS	locally weighted scatter plot smoothing
MNQ	manganese discharge
NPL	National Priorities List
NWQL	National Water Quality Laboratory
NWIS	National Water Information System
OLS	ordinary least squares
p-value	significance level
PBQ	lead discharge
Q	streamflow
R^2	coefficient of determination
RBCF	retransformation-bias-correction factor
RL	reporting level
RSD	relative standard deviation
SEDQ	suspended-sediment discharge
SE	standard error of estimate
USEPA	U.S. Environmental Protection Agency
USGS	U.S. Geological Survey
ZNQ	zinc discharge

Estimated Loads of Suspended Sediment and Selected Trace Elements Transported Through the Clark Fork Basin, Montana, in Selected Periods Before and After the Breach of Milltown Dam (Water Years 1985–2009)

By Steven K. Sando and John H. Lambing[1]

Abstract

Milltown Reservoir is a National Priorities List Superfund site in the upper Clark Fork basin of western Montana where sediments enriched in trace elements from historical mining and ore processing have been deposited since the completion of Milltown Dam in 1908. Milltown Dam was breached on March 28, 2008, as part of Superfund remediation activities to remove the dam and excavate contaminated sediment that had accumulated in Milltown Reservoir. In preparation for the breach of Milltown Dam, permanent drawdown of Milltown Reservoir began on June 1, 2006, and lowered the water-surface elevation by about 10 to 12 feet. After the breach of Milltown Dam, the water-surface elevation was lowered an additional 17 feet.

Hydrologic data-collection activities were conducted by the U.S. Geological Survey in cooperation with U.S. Environmental Protection Agency to estimate loads of suspended sediment and trace elements transported through the Clark Fork basin before and after the breach of Milltown Dam. This report presents selected results of the data-collection activities.

Daily and cumulative loads of suspended sediment and selected trace elements transported during water year 2009 were estimated for three high-intensity sampling stations that bracket the Milltown Reservoir project area and were used to quantify the net gain or loss (mass balance) of suspended sediment and trace elements within the project area for water year 2009. Estimated loads and mass balance for water year 2009 within the project area were compared to estimated loads and mass balance within the project area for selected periods before and after the breach of Milltown Dam. Loads of suspended sediment and selected trace elements transported during water years 2006–09 also were estimated for three low-intensity sampling stations in the lower Clark Fork (downstream from Milltown Reservoir project area) and were used

to evaluate how project area outflow loads were integrated into downstream transport processes.

During the period June 1, 2006 (start of permanent drawdown) to the end of water year 2009, the estimated cumulative loads contributed from within the project area were 623,000 tons, 235 tons, and 26.8 tons of suspended sediment, copper, and arsenic, respectively. During the years of the most substantial remediation activities (that is, water year 2007, when permanent drawdown was conducted for the entire year, and water year 2008 when Milltown Dam was breached), constituent loads relative to streamflow were proportionately larger than other years, and the relative contributions of constituents from within the project area also were larger than other years. The relative contributions of constituents from source areas during water years 2006 and 2009 (before and after the most substantial remediation activities) generally were similar. Thus, in a relatively short time frame after the start of the most substantial remediation activities (that is, the period from the start of permanent drawdown on June 1, 2006, to the end of water year 2008, during which two complete annual-runoff periods occurred), constituent transport characteristics in the Clark Fork near the project area appear to be approaching typical conditions observed before the breach of Milltown Dam. However, remediation and restoration activities that occur after the end of water year 2009 might affect the apparent temporal pattern in constituent transport characteristics; for example, the diversion of the Clark Fork from the constructed bypass channel to a new channel that occurred in December 2010. Adjustment of the Clark Fork to a new geomorphic environment might alter patterns in constituent transport characteristics.

The effects of the Milltown Dam removal activities are apparent in the temporal variability of relative contributions of estimated annual suspended-sediment loads from source areas to the lower Clark Fork. During the years of the most substantial remediation activities (water years 2007 and 2008), the estimated annual loads for the Clark Fork above Missoula (project area outflow) accounted for a large percentage (65 percent for water year 2007 and 70 percent

[1]U.S. Geological Survey, retired

for water year 2008) of the suspended-sediment load transported past the lower Clark Fork outflow (calculated as the sum of Clark Fork at St. Regis and Flathead River at Perma). During water years 2006 and 2009 (before and after the most substantial remediation activities), the Clark Fork above Missoula accounted for smaller percentages (25 percent for water year 2006 and 38 percent for water year 2009) of the suspended-sediment load transported past the lower Clark Fork outflow than in water years 2007–08. Also, the relative contributions of suspended sediment from source areas during water years 2006 and 2009 generally were similar.

Temporal variability in the relative contributions of estimated annual copper loads from source areas to the lower Clark Fork downstream from the project area outflow generally was similar to that of estimated annual suspended-sediment loads. During the years of the most substantial remediation activities (water years 2007 and 2008), the estimated annual loads for the project area outflow at Clark Fork above Missoula accounted for a large percentage (87 percent for water years 2007 and 2008) of the estimated annual copper load transported past the lower Clark Fork outflow. During water years 2006 and 2009 (before and after the most substantial remediation activities), the Clark Fork above Missoula accounted for a smaller percentage (60 percent for water year 2006 and 78 percent for water year 2009) of the annual copper load transported past the lower Clark Fork outflow than in water years 2007–08.

Temporal variability in the relative contributions of estimated annual arsenic loads from source areas to the lower Clark Fork differed somewhat from those of estimated annual suspended-sediment and copper loads, primarily because a relatively large proportion of arsenic is transported in dissolved phase in the Clark Fork. The project area outflow at Clark Fork above Missoula contributed about 50 percent or more of the annual arsenic load transported past the lower Clark Fork outflow for all years during 2006–09. A substantial part of the arsenic load transported past the Clark Fork above Missoula was contributed from the basin upstream from Clark Fork at Turah Bridge in all years.

For all years, loads of all constituents contributed from the basin upstream from Flathead River at Perma to the lower Clark Fork outflow generally were small, even though the Flathead River accounted for an average of 62 percent of the annual streamflow of the lower Clark Fork outflow. The interannual range in percent contribution of estimated annual loads from the Flathead River at Perma to the lower Clark Fork outflow was 5 to 19 percent for suspended sediment, 4 to 11 percent for copper, and 17 to 26 percent for arsenic.

Introduction

Milltown Reservoir was located on the Clark Fork at the confluence of the Clark Fork and Blackfoot River in western Montana (fig. 1). The reservoir was formed by the completion

of Milltown Dam in 1908 (U.S. Environmental Protection Agency, 2009) for hydroelectric power. Historical large-scale mining and ore processing in the upper Clark Fork basin produced large quantities of tailings enriched with trace elements such as cadmium, copper, lead, zinc, and arsenic. Tailings have been eroded and transported downstream along the Clark Fork, contaminating the approximately 6.6 million cubic yards (yd^3) of sediment that had accumulated in Milltown Reservoir (U.S. Environmental Protection Agency, 2004). Potential toxicity from the elevated trace-element concentrations in water and bed sediment led to the designation of Milltown Reservoir and upstream reaches of the Clark Fork as an extended National Priorities List (NPL) Superfund site in 1983 (U.S. Environmental Protection Agency, 2004).

In response to the need for a water-quality data base to guide resource management and remediation decisions, a routine data-collection program to document suspended sediment and trace elements in the upper Clark Fork basin was begun in March 1985 (Lambing, 1991) by the U.S. Geological Survey (USGS) in cooperation with the U.S. Environmental Protection Agency (USEPA) and has continued to present day (2010). The routine data-collection program is referred to in this report as the "long-term monitoring program."

As part of remediation planning associated with the Superfund process, the USEPA issued a record of decision in December 2004 that included removal of Milltown Dam as one of the remediation activities (U.S. Environmental Protection Agency, 2004). Descriptions of activities associated with the removal of Milltown Dam are provided in a series of updates by USEPA (*http://www.epa.gov/region8/superfund/mt/milltown/updates.html*, accessed October 29, 2010). On March 28, 2008, Milltown Dam was breached as part of the process to remove the dam and excavate a large portion of the contaminated sediment. The term "Milltown Reservoir project area" (hereinafter generally referred to as "project area") is used to refer to the remediation-affected area during the periods before and after the dam breach when the environment changed from a reservoir to a free-flowing river. The project area (fig. 1) collectively includes the former location of the reservoir, plus river reaches of indefinite length upstream from the Clark Fork and Blackfoot River arms of the reservoir where increased erosion could occur as the result of the rivers adjusting to the steeper hydraulic gradient caused by the breach of Milltown Dam.

To accommodate various construction activities and the excavation of a portion of the reservoir bottom sediments before dam removal, the initial phase (Stage 1) of a permanent drawdown of the reservoir to a lower pool level began on June 1, 2006 (Lambing and Sando, 2009); thus, Milltown Reservoir was relatively shallow during all of water year 2007 and part of water year 2008 before the breach of Milltown Dam. The Stage 1 drawdown lowered the average summer pool by about 10 to 12 feet (ft). Two subsequent phases of drawdown (Stages 2 and 3) were designed to lower the reservoir pool an additional 17 ft (for a total drawdown of about 29 ft) to allow access for removal of the powerhouse and

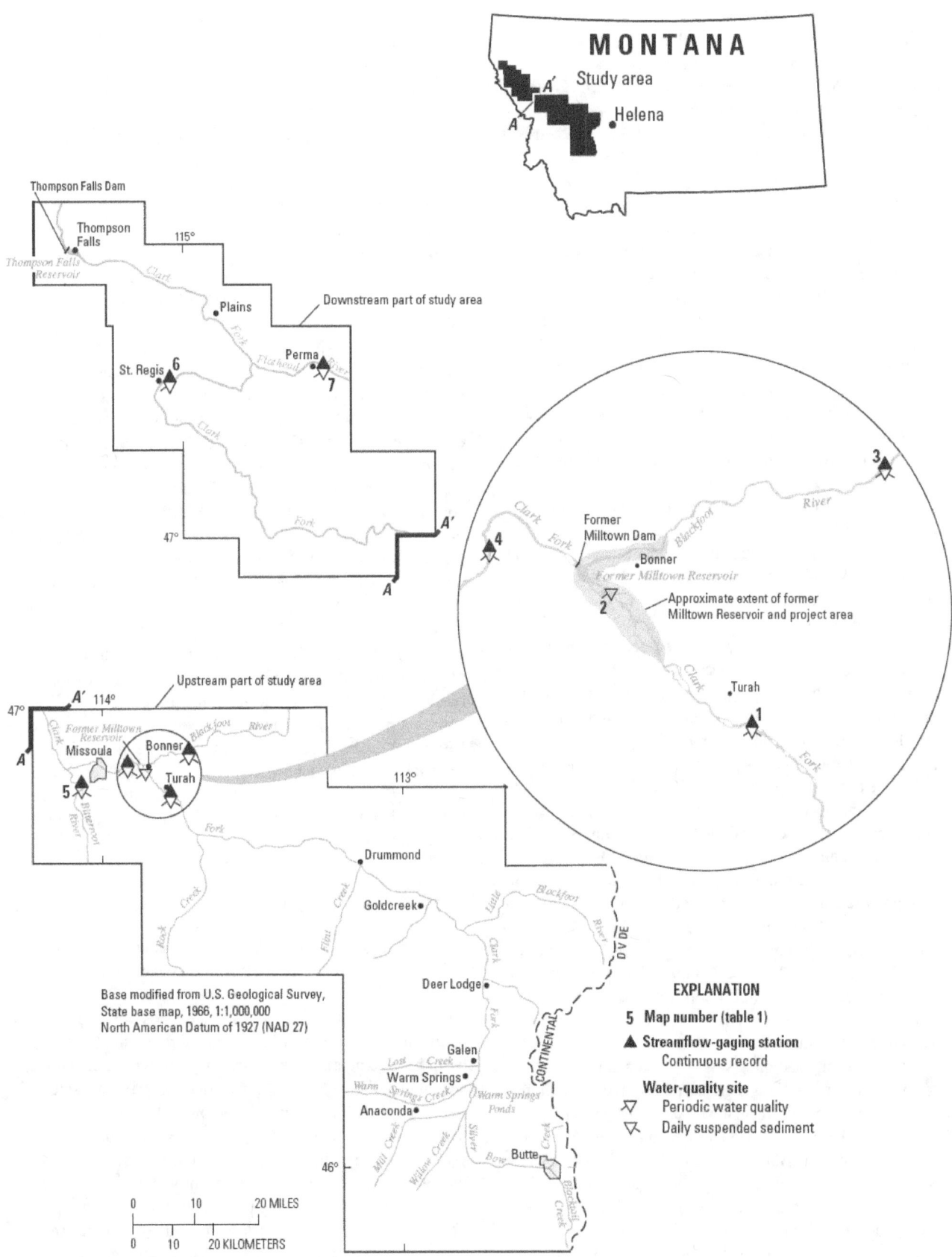

Figure 1. Location of study area.

spillway (Lambing and Sando, 2009). The Stage 2 drawdown occurred on March 28, 2008, when the powerhouse coffer dam was breached, thereby lowering the water-surface elevation by 15 ft at the former forebay foundation (*http://www. epa.gov/region8/superfund/mt/milltown/pdf/Update02Apr08. pdf*, accessed October 29, 2010). The Stage 2 drawdown is hereinafter referred to as "the breach of Milltown Dam." Prior to the breach of Milltown Dam, a bypass channel was constructed to provide controlled routing of the Clark Fork and allow further excavation of contaminated reservoir sediment for hauling to a repository. Diversion of the Clark Fork into the bypass channel began on March 21, 2008 (*http://www. epa.gov/region8/superfund/mt/milltown/pdf/Update12Mar08. pdf*, accessed October 29, 2010), and was completed with the construction of a diversion dike on the Clark Fork upstream from the bypass channel on April 12, 2008 (*http://www.epa. gov/region8/superfund/mt/milltown/pdf/Update16Apr08.pdf*, accessed October 29, 2010). The Stage 3 drawdown began when the spillway coffer dam was breached on March 27, 2009, thereby lowering the water-surface elevation the final 2 ft to the estimated pre-dam elevation at the former spillway (*http://www.epa.gov/region8/superfund/mt/milltown/pdf/ Update01Apr09.pdf*, accessed October 29, 2010).

Because of the large quantity of contaminated sediment that was deposited in Milltown Reservoir, there was concern regarding an increased potential for scour of bottom sediments and associated trace elements from the shallow reservoir after the start of the permanent drawdown, especially during high streamflow. To address this concern, the USGS in cooperation with USEPA conducted a program of intensive sampling that began in water year 2006 to supplement the routine sampling of the long-term monitoring program (Dodge and others, 2009). The supplemental sampling was conducted during the April–June periods of water years 2006 and 2007 to target the rising limb and peak flow of the annual hydrograph, as well as selected periods of reservoir drawdown. The sampling primarily provided additional information on variations in water quality and constituent transport through Milltown Reservoir. The supplemental sampling continued in March–July of water years 2008–09 to characterize suspended-sediment and trace-element transport during (1) the final stages of the permanent reservoir drawdown, (2) the period immediately before and after the breach of Milltown Dam in water year 2008, and (3) the runoff period of water year 2009, about 1 year after the breach of Milltown Dam.

High-intensity sampling was conducted at three streamflow-gaging stations (hereinafter referred to as "high-intensity stations"; table 1) that bracket the project area. Clark Fork at Turah Bridge, near Bonner (station 12334550) and Blackfoot River near Bonner (station 12340000) are upstream from the project area and represent the primary inflows to the project area. Clark Fork above Missoula (station 12340500) is downstream from the project area and represents the outflow from the project area. Daily loads for these stations were estimated by using periodic water-quality, daily streamflow, and daily suspended-sediment data. Annual loads for selected periods were determined by summing estimated daily loads for each site. The difference between the annual inflow and outflow loads were used to quantify the net gain or loss (mass balance) of suspended sediment and selected trace elements within the project area.

Although the supplemental sampling primarily focused on the three high-intensity stations that bracket the Milltown Reservoir project area and the transport of suspended-sediment and trace-element loads to and from the project area, low-intensity sampling also was conducted at four other stations (hereinafter referred to as "low-intensity stations"; table 1). Periodic water-quality samples were collected at Clark Fork Bypass near Bonner (station 12334570) in water years 2008–09 to provide information on the erosional processes occurring within the former Milltown Reservoir as the river adjusted to the steeper channel gradient caused by the breach of Milltown Dam. The Clark Fork Bypass did not have a continuous streamflow gage, and flows were considered equivalent to those at Clark Fork at Turah Bridge. Suspended-sediment data for the periodic water-quality samples collected at Clark Fork Bypass near Bonner are compared with concurrently collected data at Clark Fork at Turah Bridge to provide information on suspended-sediment transport within the intervening reach. Periodic water-quality samples also were collected in water years 2006–09 at three low-intensity stations in the Clark Fork basin downstream from Clark Fork above Missoula (station 12340500; the outflow from the project area) to provide general information on the transport of suspended-sediment and trace-element loads to and from reaches of the Clark Fork between the project area outflow and just downstream from the confluence with the Flathead River (hereinafter referred to as the lower Clark Fork). The three low-intensity stations downstream from the project area outflow are Bitterroot River near Missoula (station 12352500), Clark Fork at St. Regis (station 12354500), and Flathead River at Perma (station 12388700).

Purpose and Scope

The purpose of this report is to present selected results of hydrologic data-collection activities conducted by the U.S. Geological Survey, in cooperation with U.S. Environmental Protection Agency, to estimate loads of suspended sediment and trace elements transported through the Clark Fork basin before and after the breach of Milltown Dam. Daily and annual cumulative loads of suspended sediment and selected trace elements (unfiltered-recoverable cadmium, copper, iron, lead, manganese, zinc, and arsenic) transported during water year 2009 were estimated for three high-intensity stations that bracket the Milltown Reservoir project area (fig. 1). The annual estimated loads were used to quantify the mass balance of suspended sediment and trace elements within the project area for water year 2009. Estimated loads and mass balance within the project area for water year 2009 are compared to estimated loads and mass balance within the project area

Table 1. Data-collection stations and information on data-collection activities in the study area during water years 1985–2009.

[Abbreviations: e, estimated from U.S. Geological Survey 7.5-minute topographic map. Symbols: --, no data collected. For map number location, see figure 1]

Map number	Station number	Station name	Drainage area (square miles)	Data-collection intensity designation	Information on data-collection activities		
					Water years of continuous streamflow data collection	Water years of daily suspended-sediment data collection	Water years of periodic water-quality sampling data collection (average number of samples per year)
1	12334550	Clark Fork at Turah Bridge, near Bonner, Mont.	3,641	High intensity	1986–2009	1985–2009	1985–2005 (9); 2006–09 (22)
2	12334570	Clark Fork Bypass, near Bonner, Mont.	e3,650	Low intensity	--	--	2008–09 (14)[1]
3	12340000	Blackfoot River near Bonner, Mont.	2,290	High intensity	1985–2009	1986–95, 2006–09	1985–2005 (5); 2006–09 (20)
4	12340500	Clark Fork above Missoula, Mont.	5,999	High intensity	1985–2009	1986–2009	1990–2005 (10); 2006–09 (22)
5	12352500	Bitterroot River near Missoula, Mont.	2,814	Low intensity	1989–2009	--	2006–09 (14)[1]
6	12354500	Clark Fork at St. Regis, Mont.	10,709	Low intensity	1985–2009	--	2006–09 (14)[1]
7	12388700	Flathead River at Perma, Mont.	8,795	Low intensity	1985–2009	--	2006–09 (14)[1]

[1]Samples collected seasonally, generally from March–July.

for selected periods before and after the breach of Milltown Dam, including (1) long-term average annual values for water years 1985–2005 (representing long-term average conditions during the period before the start of permanent drawdown of Milltown Reservoir on June 1, 2006), (2) average annual values for 1996–97 (representing high-streamflow conditions during the period before the start of permanent drawdown of Milltown Reservoir on June 1, 2006), (3) water years 2006–07 (representing the period between the start of permanent drawdown of Milltown Reservoir and the breach of Milltown Dam), and (4) water year 2008 (the year when Milltown Dam was breached). In this report, emphasis often is placed on differences in constituent transport between water year 2008 (the year when Milltown Dam was breached) and water year 2009 (the first complete water year after the dam breach).

Estimated suspended-sediment and trace-element loads for three low-intensity stations for water years 2006–09 also are presented in this report to provide general information on the transport of suspended-sediment and trace-element loads to and from reaches of the lower Clark Fork downstream from the project area outflow. Because data-collection activities were less intensive for the low-intensity stations than for the high-intensity stations, the presentation of results for the low-intensity stations is limited and load estimates are less confident than load estimates for high-intensity stations. For the

low-intensity stations, emphasis generally is placed on relative comparison of load estimates and transport patterns between stations and between years, rather than on the absolute magnitudes of load estimates.

The methods used to estimate loads for the high-intensity and low-intensity sampling stations are described. The hydrologic data, including streamflow and constituent concentrations, used to estimate loads (or presented in support of the load estimates and interpretive conclusions) are accessible on the USGS National Water Information System (NWIS) Web site for Montana (*http://waterdata.usgs.gov/mt/nwis*). Load estimates presented in this report represent water-column transport of constituents and do not include bedload transport.

Description of the Study Area

Milltown Reservoir was a small impoundment (surface area of about 540 acres) formed by Milltown Dam just downstream from the confluence of the Clark Fork and Blackfoot River (fig. 1). The Clark Fork basin upstream from Milltown Dam drains an area of about 6,000 square miles (mi²). The Clark Fork basin upstream from the confluence with the Blackfoot River accounts for about 61 percent (about 3,650 mi²) of the drainage area upstream from the former Milltown Dam. The Blackfoot River at the mouth accounts for about 38 percent (about 2,280 mi²) of the drainage area upstream from the former Milltown Dam. The former reservoir was at the downstream end of a contiguous complex of NPL Superfund sites (established for remediation of effects of large-scale mining operations) extending from the headwaters of Silver Bow Creek near Butte to Milltown Dam near Missoula (U.S. Environmental Protection Agency, 2004). In the Blackfoot River basin, numerous small-scale placer and hard-rock mining operations have been active since about 1865 (Moore and others, 1991).

Before the breach of Milltown Dam, Milltown Reservoir was considered a "run-of-the-river" reservoir because on a daily basis streamflow leaving the reservoir generally was about equal to the streamflow of the Clark Fork and Blackfoot River entering the reservoir (Lambing and Sando, 2009), where the retention time of water in the reservoir generally was not substantially different than a free-flowing system. After Milltown Dam was breached, the confluence of the Clark Fork and Blackfoot River transitioned from a reservoir environment to a free-flowing river.

The study area includes the Clark Fork basin from near Butte to Thompson Falls Dam (fig. 1). Data for two high-intensity stations upstream from the Milltown Reservoir project area (Clark Fork at Turah Bridge, near Bonner, station 12334550; and Blackfoot River near Bonner, station 12340000) represent the combined inflow of streamflow and constituent load to the project area; data for the high-intensity station Clark Fork above Missoula (station 12340500) represent the outflow from the project area. For brevity, Clark Fork at Turah Bridge, near Bonner is referred to as Clark Fork at Turah Bridge in this report. The low-intensity station within the project area (Clark Fork Bypass near Bonner, station 12334570) is located about 5 river mi downstream from Clark Fork at Turah Bridge (table 1 and fig. 1). This low-intensity station is near the upstream end of a constructed bypass channel into which the Clark Fork started to be diverted on March 21, 2008, to allow the excavation of contaminated reservoir sediment for hauling to a repository (*http://www.epa.gov/region8/superfund/mt/milltown/pdf/ Update12Mar08.pdf, accessed October 29, 2010*).

Data for three low-intensity stations provide information on the transport of suspended-sediment and trace-element loads to and from reaches of the Clark Fork downstream from the project area outflow. Bitterroot River near Missoula (station 12352500) is located about 5 river mi upstream from the mouth of the Bitterroot River. The confluence of the Bitterroot River with the Clark Fork is located about 11 river mi downstream from Clark Fork above Missoula. Clark Fork at St. Regis (station 12354500) is located about 87 river mi downstream from the high-intensity station Clark Fork above Missoula and about 24 river mi upstream from the confluence of the Clark Fork and the Flathead River. Flathead River at Perma (station 12388700) is located about 11 river mi upstream from the mouth of the Flathead River. The confluence of the Flathead River with the Clark Fork is located about 45 river mi upstream from Thompson Falls Dam.

The main-stem reach of the Clark Fork from Clark Fork above Missoula (the project area outflow) to Clark Fork at St. Regis serves as an accounting area downstream from the project area outflow for determination of annual mass balance of suspended sediment and selected trace elements. Mass-balance estimates for this reach can be used to evaluate how project area outflow loads were incorporated into downstream transport processes. Data for the high-intensity station Clark Fork above Missoula and the low-intensity station Bitter-root River near Missoula represent the primary inflows to the reach; data for the low-intensity station Clark Fork at St. Regis represents the outflow from the main-stem reach above the Flathead River.

Suspended-sediment and trace-element loads transported in the Clark Fork to Thompson Falls Reservoir also are of significance in evaluating the effects of the removal of Milltown Dam. The combined streamflows and constituent loads of Clark Fork at St. Regis and Flathead River at Perma represent both the total outflow from the lower Clark Fork and the primary inflow to Thompson Falls Reservoir.

Hydrologic Characteristics

Streamflow magnitude is a predominant factor affecting the transport of suspended sediment and sediment-associated constituents through a drainage basin. Streamflow magnitude can affect the sustained delivery of constituent loads from the basin, as well as the capacity to locally scour sediments within the project area. The hydraulic energy associated with high flows is especially important relative to the scour of bottom sediments in shallow-water bodies, such as Milltown Reservoir during the permanent drawdown period. Increased hydraulic energy from high flows and the steeper hydraulic gradient after the breach of Milltown Dam are primary factors affecting erosion of remnant coffer dam materials, former reservoir bottom sediments, and channel streambed and banks.

Because streamflow can vary substantially from year to year, thereby affecting rates of constituent transport, comparison of streamflow during water years 2004–09 to a long-term period of record allows recent hydrologic conditions to be placed in a historical perspective. Clark Fork above Missoula has the longest period of continuous-streamflow record in the upper Clark Fork basin (80 years, water years 1930–2009) for comparison to streamflow during water years 2004–09. The variation in daily mean streamflow at Clark Fork above Missoula during water years 2004–09 is shown in figure 2, along with selected long-term streamflow characteristics for water years 1930–2009, to illustrate differences between recent and long-term hydrologic conditions. Water years 2004–09 are specifically presented in figure 2 to illustrate streamflow conditions before the start of permanent drawdown, during permanent drawdown, the day that Milltown Dam was breached, and the period after the breach of Milltown Dam.

The long-term streamflow characteristics for Clark Fork above Missoula (fig. 2) are represented by selected exceedance percentiles (10th, 50th, and 90th) of daily mean streamflow during the period of record (water years 1930–2009). An exceedance percentile indicates the magnitude of daily mean streamflow that was exceeded the given percent of time on a specific day of the year during the long-term period of record. For example, the 10th-exceedance percentile of long-term daily mean streamflow represents a relatively high stream-flow magnitude that was exceeded only 10 percent of the time on that specific day of the year (for example, on all of the October 1 dates, October 2 dates, and so on) during the period of record. Exceedance percentiles are determined for each day of the year to produce an annual hydrograph of long-term daily mean streamflows representing a particular exceedance percentile (hereinafter referred to as percentile). For brevity and relative comparison of streamflow during water years 2004–09 to long-term streamflow, "normal" in this report refers to the 50th percentile, or long-term median.

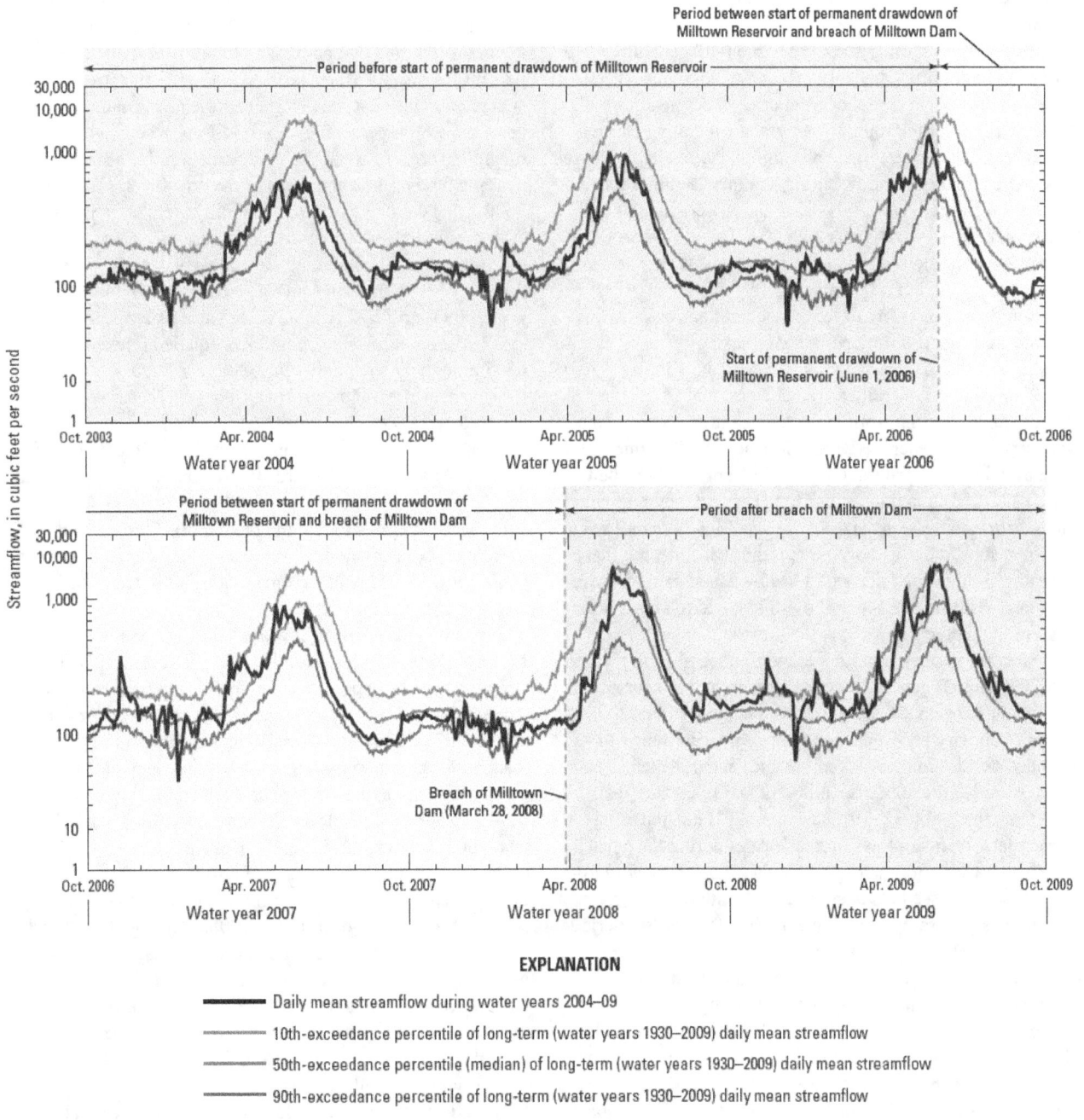

EXPLANATION

——— Daily mean streamflow during water years 2004–09

——— 10th-exceedance percentile of long-term (water years 1930–2009) daily mean streamflow

——— 50th-exceedance percentile (median) of long-term (water years 1930–2009) daily mean streamflow

——— 90th-exceedance percentile of long-term (water years 1930–2009) daily mean streamflow

Figure 2. Daily mean streamflow during water year 2004–09 and selected exceedance percentiles of long-term (water years 1930–2009) daily mean streamflow for Clark Fork above Missoula, Mont.

Streamflow conditions associated with suspended-sediment and trace-element loads reported for 1985–97 are reported in Lambing (1991), Hornberger and others (1997), and Lambing (1998). Descriptions of streamflow conditions during water years 2004–08 are presented in Lambing and Sando (2008, 2009). Streamflow conditions during water years 2004–08 are briefly summarized in this report to provide information on factors affecting constituent transport before the start of permanent drawdown, during permanent drawdown, and after the breach of Milltown Dam. Detailed descriptions of streamflow conditions during water year 2009 with specific comparisons to streamflow conditions during water year 2008 also are presented.

Streamflows during water years 2004–07 generally were below or near normal at Clark Fork above Missoula (fig. 2). Although the annual peak flows generally were near normal, the falling limb of the runoff hydrograph generally occurred sooner relative to long-term conditions and typically decreased to below-normal streamflow during summer. Summer streamflows during water years 2004–07 at times were near or at the 90th percentile. In water years 2006–07, the below-normal streamflow conditions continued into the fall. Winter streamflows were erratic in most years, possibly due to variations in the duration and intensity of freezing conditions or snowfall amounts and runoff during periods of thawing.

Streamflows at Clark Fork above Missoula during water year 2008 (fig. 2) generally were below normal from about October 2007 through April 2008. Winter streamflows again were erratic, but generally were below normal. Sustained runoff started in mid-April (after Milltown Dam was breached on March 28), and streamflows rose to near normal by mid-May and to substantially above normal by late May. Streamflows remained substantially above normal through June, but the departure from normal decreased in July and streamflows were near normal in August. Streamflows increased to above normal again in September.

Streamflows at Clark Fork above Missoula during water year 2009 (fig. 2) generally were above normal to near normal throughout the year. Streamflows from about October 2008 through February 2009 generally were above normal with extended periods in mid-November and January when streamflows exceeded the 10th percentile. Six days in water year 2009 (November 14–17, 19, and January 14) had the maximum recorded streamflows for those dates during the period of record at Clark Fork above Missoula (*http://waterdata.usgs.gov/mt/nwis* accessed October 29, 2010). Although winter streamflows generally were above normal, there was a period during late December when streamflows decreased sharply to less than the 90th percentile. December 16 had the minimum recorded streamflow for that date during the period of record at Clark Fork above Missoula. Streamflows from about March through early June generally ranged from near normal to substantially above normal. There were 18 days during the rising limb of the runoff hydrograph when streamflow equaled or exceeded the 10th percentile. Starting in early June 2009, streamflows declined sharply to near-normal levels and continued at generally near-normal levels through the remainder of the water year. There were, however, several days in late August when streamflows exceeded the 10th percentile. As in water year 2008, the timing of the rising limb, peak flow, and falling limb of the runoff hydrograph generally was similar to long-term patterns, unlike the pronounced shift towards an earlier occurrence of runoff and recession noted for water years 2006 and 2007.

Differences in rising-limb streamflows between water year 2009 and water year 2008 are of particular relevance to differences in suspended-sediment and trace-element transport between the two years. Differences in rising-limb streamflows between water year 2009 and water year 2008 are best discerned by comparison to the 10th, 50th, and 90th percentiles (fig. 2). Water year 2008 rising-limb streamflows started at levels near the 90th percentile and remained below or near the 50th percentile until mid-May when there was a precipitous rise to about the 10th percentile for a short period near the time of the annual peak flow on May 21. Water year 2009 rising-limb streamflows generally were at or above the 50th percentile with some extended periods near or above the 10th percentile including several days near the time of the annual peak flow on May 31. Near the peak of the water year 2009 runoff hydrograph, there were 8 consecutive days (May 25–June 1) when streamflows equaled or exceeded the maximum daily streamflow in water year 2008.

Annual streamflow and peak-flow characteristics for selected periods (table 2) for Clark Fork above Missoula are compared to long-term characteristics for the period of continuous-streamflow records (water years 1930–2009) and peak-flow records (water years 1908, 1930–2009). Characteristics for the periods before the breach of Milltown Dam are presented for informational purposes. Characteristics for water years 2008–09 and comparisons to long-term characteristics are discussed in more detail.

Annual mean streamflow at Clark Fork above Missoula for water year 2008 [3,040 cubic feet per second (ft^3/s)] was slightly larger (105 percent) than the long-term mean annual streamflow (2,910 ft^3/s). Annual mean streamflow for water year 2009 (3,560 ft^3/s) was substantially larger (122 percent) than the long-term mean annual streamflow and also moderately larger than the water year 2008 annual mean streamflow. The annual peak flows for water year 2008 and water year 2009 were identical (17,500 ft^3/s) and were 112 percent of the long-term mean annual peak flow (15,600 ft^3/s), but only 36 percent of the long-term maximum annual peak flow (48,000 ft^3/s), which occurred in 1908. Although the annual peak flows for water year 2008 and water year 2009 were identical, streamflows in water year 2009 remained near the annual peak flow magnitude for several days before and after the peak flow, whereas the rise to and fall from the annual peak flow was more precipitous in water year 2008.

Annual streamflow and peak-flow characteristics for the individual water years 2006–09 (table 3) for Clark Fork at St. Regis are compared to long-term characteristics for the period of continuous-streamflow records and peak-flow records (water years 1911–23, 1929–2009). Streamflow characteristics for Clark Fork at St. Regis provide information relevant to suspended-sediment and trace-element transport characteristics for the Clark Fork basin downstream from the project area outflow.

Annual mean streamflows at Clark Fork at St. Regis for water years 2006–07 (6,560 and 6,040 ft³/s, respectively) were smaller (90 and 83 percent, respectively) than the long-term mean annual streamflow (7,280 ft³/s). Annual mean streamflows for water years 2008–09 (7,610 and 7,810 ft³/s, respectively) were similar in magnitude and were slightly larger (104 and 107 percent, respectively) than the long-term mean annual streamflow. The annual peak flow for water year 2006 (39,600 ft³/s) was slightly larger (107 percent) than the long-term mean peak flow (37,000 ft³/s), and the annual peak flow for water year 2007 (23,600 ft³/s) was substantially smaller (64 percent) than the long-term mean peak flow. The annual peak flows for water year 2008 and water year 2009 (46,300 and 42,700 ft³/s, respectively) were substantially to moderately larger (125 and 115 percent, respectively) than the long-term mean annual peak flow, but were only 67 and 62 percent of the long-term maximum annual peak flow (68,900 ft³/s), which occurred in 1948.

Methods of Data Collection and Quality Assurance

Methods of data collection associated with suspended-sediment and trace-element loads reported for the high-intensity stations for water years 1985–97 are reported in Lambing (1991), Hornberger and others (1997), and Lambing (1998). Methods of data collection associated with suspended-sediment and trace-element loads reported for water years 2004–08 are presented in Lambing and Sando (2008, 2009). Methods of data collection for the high-intensity stations during water year 2009 are presented in this report.

Constituent loads for the low-intensity stations have not been previously estimated or reported. Data-collection activities for the low-intensity stations were restricted to water years 2006–09, and the data-collection methods are presented in this report.

Water-quality samples were collected periodically for analysis of suspended sediment and trace elements. Routine samples at the three high-intensity stations bracketing the Milltown Reservoir project area (table 1, fig. 1) were collected at a frequency of 6 to 8 times during water year 2009 as part

Table 2. Annual streamflow and peak-flow characteristics for selected periods, with comparison to long-term annual streamflow (water years 1930–2009) and peak-flow (water years 1908, 1930–2009) characteristics for Clark Fork above Missoula, Mont. (station 12340500).

[Abbreviations: ft³/s, cubic feet per second]

Water year(s)	Annual streamflow			Annual peak flow		
	Annual mean streamflow (ft³/s)	Percent of long-term mean annual streamflow (2,910 ft³/s)	Percent of long-term maximum annual streamflow (5,070 ft³/s; 1976)	Annual peak flow (ft³/s)	Percent of long-term mean peak flow (15,600 ft³/s)	Percent of long-term maximum peak flow (48,000 ft³/s; 1908)
Period before start of permanent drawdown of Milltown Reservoir on June 1, 2006 (water years 1985–2005)						
1985–2005[1,2]	2,550	88	50	12,200	78	25
1996-97[1,3]	4,540	156	90	22,800	146	47
Period between start of permanent drawdown of Milltown Reservoir on June 1, 2006, and breach of Milltown Dam on March 28, 2008 (water years 2006–07)						
2006[4]	2,480	86	49	12,900	83	27
2007	2,440	84	48	9,320	60	19
Period after breach of Milltown Dam on March 28, 2008 (water years 2008–09)						
2008[4]	3,040	105	60	17,500	112	36
2009	3,560	122	70	17,500	112	36

[1]Average values for the indicated period (mean annual).

[2]Average values for water years 1985–2005 represent typical conditions during the period before the start of permanent drawdown of Milltown Reservoir.

[3]Average values for water years 1996–97 represent high-flow conditions during the period before the start of permanent drawdown of Milltown Reservoir.

[4]Although part of the given water year occurred outside of the indicated period, the given water year is assigned to the period most representative of the prevailing conditions of that water year.

Table 3. Annual streamflow and peak-flow characteristics for selected periods, with comparison to long-term annual streamflow and peak-flow (water years 1911–23, 1929–2009) characteristics for Clark Fork at St. Regis, Mont. (station 12354500).

[Abbreviations: ft³/s, cubic feet per second]

Water year(s)	Annual streamflow			Annual peak flow		
	Annual mean streamflow (ft³/s)	Percent of long-term mean annual streamflow (7,280 ft³/s)	Percent of long-term maximum annual streamflow (11,600 ft³/s; 1997)	Annual peak flow (ft³/s)	Percent of long-term mean peak flow (37,000 ft³/s)	Percent of long-term maximum peak flow (68,900 ft³/s; 1948)
Period between start of permanent drawdown of Milltown Reservoir on June 1, 2006, and breach of Milltown Dam on March 28, 2008 (water years 2006–07)						
2006[1]	6,560	90	57	39,600	107	57
2007	6,040	83	52	23,600	64	34
Period after breach of Milltown Dam on March 28, 2008 (water years 2008–09)						
2008[1]	7,610	104	66	46,300	125	67
2009	7,810	107	68	42,700	115	62

[1]Although part of the given water year occurred outside of the indicated period, the given water year is assigned to the period most representative of the prevailing conditions of that water year.

of the long-term Clark Fork monitoring program (Dodge and others, 2009). The routine long-term samples were collected during both runoff and base-flow periods. An additional 19 samples were collected at each of the three high-intensity stations during the runoff period of the annual hydrograph (March–July) of water year 2009 as part of a supplemental monitoring program for the lower Clark Fork basin. These additional samples provide better resolution of the transport of sediment and trace elements from the project area associated with dam-removal activities and high-flow conditions when most of the annual transport was expected to occur. The combined sampling efforts for both programs resulted in a sampling frequency of 25 to 27 times in water year 2009 at each of the high-intensity stations.

The four low-intensity stations (table 1, fig. 1) are not part of the long-term monitoring program, and periodic water-quality samples were not collected at these sites before the start of the supplemental monitoring program in water year 2006. For three of the low-intensity stations in the lower Clark Fork (Bitterroot River near Missoula, Clark Fork at St. Regis, and Flathead River at Perma), periodic water-quality sampling was started in water year 2006. For Clark Fork Bypass near Bonner (located within the Milltown Reservoir project area), periodic water-quality sampling was started in water year 2008. The sampling frequency for each of the low-intensity stations ranged from 11 to 21 times per year during water years 2006–09, with samples collected seasonally during the runoff period (March–July).

Generally, periodic water-quality samples were collected by the USGS throughout the entire stream depth at multiple locations across the stream by using depth- and width-integration methods described by Ward and Harr (1990), Edwards and Glysson (1999), and U.S. Geological Survey (variously dated). However, the use of standard depth- and width-integrating procedures for the Clark Fork Bypass were not practical, because the steep gradient of the channel and the routing of the water through the openings between the bridge piers resulted in areas of turbulence, eddying, and unrepresentative flow direction such that sampling locations could not be distributed uniformly across the stream. Thus, for the Clark Fork Bypass, depth-integrated water samples were collected at 3 to 4 locations across the stream in areas of substantial discharge with generally uniform and representative flow direction.

Sampling equipment consisted of depth-integrating suspended-sediment samplers (DH–81, D–74TM, and D–95), which were equipped with nylon nozzles and constructed of plastic or coated with a nonmetallic epoxy paint. Depth-integrating samplers are designed to sample the water column isokinetically, whereby velocity flow paths into the nozzle are not distorted and suspended particles enter the sample-collection bottle at the same concentration as in the surrounding water. The samplers collect water from the water surface to the top of an unsampled zone about 4 inches above the streambed; however, bedload materials transported below the unsampled zone are not sampled by depth-integrating suspended-sediment samplers. The combination of appropriate sampling methods and depth-integrating sampling equipment provides a vertically and laterally discharge-weighted composite sample of water and suspended-particulate matter that is representative of the flow passing through the cross-sectional area of the stream. Samples were processed onsite according to procedures described by Ward and Harr (1990), Horowitz and others (1994), and U.S. Geological Survey (variously dated). Quality-assurance procedures for processing water-quality samples are described by U.S. Geological Survey (variously dated) and Lambing (2006).

Measurements of pH, specific conductance, and water temperature were collected onsite during all sampling visits. Generally, instantaneous streamflow at the time of periodic water-quality sampling was determined either by direct measurement at the time of sampling or from stage readings applied to the stage-discharge rating table for the station (Rantz and others, 1982). However, because a continuous streamflow-gaging station was not operated at the low-intensity station Clark Fork Bypass near Bonner and streamflow could not be accurately measured at this site, streamflow at the time of sampling was not directly determined. Instead, streamflow at Clark Fork Bypass was assumed to be equal to the streamflow determined for Clark Fork at Turah Bridge, located about 5 mi upstream.

Daily mean streamflows at the sampling stations with continuous streamflow gages were determined by applying stage-discharge relations developed from periodic streamflow measurements to the continuous record of stage according to procedures described by Rantz and others (1982). The three high-intensity stations also were operated as daily-sediment stations during water year 2009. Suspended-sediment samples for the daily-sediment stations were collected at a high frequency (2 to 14 times per week) by local contract observers using depth-integration methods at a single location near midstream. The frequency of suspended-sediment sample collection by observers increased seasonally as flows increased or temporarily during short-duration periods of runoff. Quality-assurance procedures for generating daily records of streamflow and suspended-sediment data are described by White and others (1998). The quality of daily records (Rantz and others, 1982) were rated good to excellent, except for periods of ice cover, which were rated poor.

Periodic water-quality samples were analyzed for suspended-sediment concentration and percent of suspended sediment finer than 0.062-mm diameter by the USGS Montana Water Science Center Sediment Laboratory (hereinafter referred to as Montana Sediment Laboratory) in Helena, Mont., according to methods described by Guy (1969) and Dodge and Lambing (2006). Samples collected by observers for the daily sediment stations were analyzed only for suspended-sediment concentration. Quality-assurance procedures used by the Montana Sediment Laboratory are described by Dodge and Lambing (2006).

Periodic water-quality samples also were analyzed for filtered (0.45-μm pore size) and unfiltered-recoverable trace-element concentrations by the USGS National Water Quality Laboratory (NWQL) in Denver, Colo. Filtered concentrations formerly were referred to as dissolved (Lambing, 1991; Lambing, 1998; Hornberger and others, 1997); unfiltered-recoverable concentrations formerly were referred to as total recoverable. Unfiltered-recoverable concentrations represent the combined dissolved and particulate fractions of the trace element. Unfiltered samples were first digested with dilute hydrochloric acid before analysis to liberate the weakly bound trace elements from sediment particles (Hoffman and others, 1996). Filtered samples and the digested unfiltered samples

then were analyzed by inductively coupled plasma–mass spectrometry (Garbarino and Struzeski, 1998). Quality-assurance procedures used by the NWQL are described by Friedman and Erdmann (1982), Jones (1987), Pritt and Raese (1995), and Maloney (2005).

Quality-assurance data for periodic water-quality samples were obtained by analysis of quality-control samples (blanks and replicates), which were submitted along with the environmental samples on every field trip. Analytical results for quality-control samples are used to evaluate the performance of sampling and analytical methods to ensure that results for environmental samples are accurate and unbiased. Quality-assurance data for the long-term Clark Fork basin sampling program are reported in annual data reports for previous years; quality-assurance data for water year 2009 are available for inspection (Dodge and others, 2010).

Trace-element concentrations in blank samples collected during water years 2006–09 were almost always less than the reporting level (RL). Values exceeding twice the RL were noted during data reviews to evaluate the presence of a consistent trend that could indicate systematic contamination. Values exceeding twice the RL were infrequent (only 2 occurrences for zinc in about 650 individual analyses for all trace elements) and occurred sporadically, which indicated that there were no consistent trends of contamination bias that might affect the data for environmental samples; therefore, no adjustments to trace-element concentrations were made during water years 2006–09 based on analytical results for blanks.

Precision of trace-element concentrations was determined by calculating a relative standard deviation (RSD) for analytical results of replicate samples. The RSD is calculated according to the following equation (Taylor, 1987):

$$RSD = \frac{S}{\bar{x}} \times 100, \qquad (1)$$

where

RSD is the relative standard deviation;

S is the standard deviation; and

$\bar{x}$ is the mean concentration for all replicate analyses.

The RSDs for all the unfiltered-recoverable trace elements used to estimate loads during water years 2006–09 were within the 20-percent data quality objective of acceptable precision for concentrations in replicate samples, with the exception of iron in water year 2008 replicate samples and copper, lead, and manganese in water year 2009 samples. The RSD for the water year 2008 iron-replicate samples was 30 percent. The high RSD resulted from poor agreement for a single replicate sample pair; removing the results for the problem replicate pair resulted in a low RSD of 6 percent. The RSD for the water year 2009 copper, lead, and manganese replicate samples ranged from 22 to 46 percent and resulted from poor agreement for a single replicate sample pair; removing the results for the problem replicate pair resulted in low RSDs ranging from 5.1 to 12 percent. Thus, the replicate samples indicate acceptable precision, and the infrequent problem replicates represent isolated occurrences rather than systematic sampling or analytical problems.

Methods for Estimating Constituent Loads

The term "load" represents the mass (commonly expressed as tons) of a constituent transported past a sampling site during a specified period of time. Loads can be computed for various time increments, such as instantaneous, daily, monthly, seasonal, or annual. Instantaneous loads represent the mass transported at the time of sampling, whereas daily, monthly, seasonal, and annual loads represent the cumulative mass transported over a prolonged period. The term "discharge" represents the rate at which load is transported and incorporates both mass and time units (commonly expressed as tons per day or tons per year). The measured instantaneous discharge of a constituent is calculated as the product of sample concentration and instantaneous streamflow at the time of sampling. Instantaneous discharge also can be expressed as an equivalent daily discharge that represents the total load transported during a day (daily load) assuming that the measured rate of instantaneous discharge was maintained for 24 hours. Daily loads can be added to determine the cumulative load for specific periods within a year or an annual load for the entire year.

Cumulative load estimates, such as seasonal or annual, generally are more informative than instantaneous loads measured at the time of sampling because they represent the total constituent mass transported over a prolonged period, and thereby incorporate the potentially large range of daily and seasonal variations. Further, load estimates associated with short periods (such as instantaneous or daily periods) can have relatively large errors, but such errors generally are about equally distributed in the negative and positive direction. Summing short-period load estimates to produce cumulative load estimates for a longer period generally results in smaller relative errors for the longer term period due to balancing of negative and positive errors associated with the short-period load estimates. Cumulative load estimates also are useful for evaluating differences in constituent transport among sites to identify source areas contributing substantial inputs on a sustained basis over time. Differences in cumulative loads transported past various locations along a stream can result from differences in seasonal or annual flow volumes, physical basin characteristics, current and historical land-use activities, and localized conditions that affect constituent supply or susceptibility to erosion.

Estimation of cumulative loads typically requires either high-frequency sampling or applying statistical relations, such as regression equations (Cohn and others, 1992), to a daily record of a hydrologically related explanatory variable to produce an estimated daily load. The daily loads estimated by

such methods provide increased temporal resolution of variability within a year that can give added insight to the effects of streamflow variations, seasonal differences, or unique conditions associated with discrete events.

Methods for developing regression equations used to estimate constituent loads reported for the high-intensity stations for water years 1985–97 are reported in Lambing (1991), Hornberger and others (1997), and Lambing (1998). Methods for developing regression equations used to estimate constituent loads reported for water years 2004–08 are presented in Lambing and Sando (2008, 2009). Methods for developing regression equations used to estimate constituent loads for the high-intensity stations during water year 2009 are presented in this report.

Constituent loads for the low-intensity stations have not been previously estimated or reported. Methods for developing regression equations used to estimate constituent loads for the low-intensity stations during water years 2006–09 are presented in this report.

Regression equations used to estimate constituent discharges based on relations with explanatory variables were developed from instantaneous streamflow at the time of sampling and concentration data for periodic water-quality samples collected during all or part of water years 2004–09. Various forms of data transformation were examined to produce a linear distribution that could be fit adequately by an ordinary least squares (OLS) regression line (Helsel and Hirsch, 2002). Selection of the best data transformation was based on the ability to produce linear relations that were statistically significant at the 0.05 significance level (p-value <0.05) and that had a uniform distribution of residuals around the regression line. Also, the coefficient of determination (R^2) and standard error of estimate (SE), in percent, which are measures of the scatter of data points around the regression line, were used in conjunction with statistical significance and uniformity of residual distribution to evaluate the various relations and select the best form of regression equation.

Some trace-element concentrations were censored (reported as less than the RL) for nearly all stations (table 4). In previous reports presenting estimated loads of trace elements for the high-intensity stations (Lambing, 1991; Lambing, 1998; Hornberger and others, 1997; Lambing and Sando, 2008, 2009), trace-element concentrations that were censored were estimated by substituting one-half of the RL that was in effect during the data-collection period. For constituents that had multiple RLs during the data-collection period, one-half of the median RL during the period was substituted. Data analysis indicated that this approach for handling censored concentrations was suitable for meeting the study objectives (Lambing and Sando, 2009) and did not substantially bias the study results. However, load estimates for constituents having greater than about 30-percent censored concentrations for a given site were qualified as having greater uncertainty than constituents with no or a very small percent of censored concentrations.

A more rigorous method of estimating censored concentrations [Adjusted Maximum Likelihood Estimation (AMLE) regression; Helsel and Hirsch, 2002] was used in this report for water year 2009 data for the high-intensity stations and water years 2006–09 data for the low-intensity stations. Justification for using AMLE regression for these data, detailed description of the application of the method, and general comparisons between results of the AMLE regression method and results of the substitution method are provided in Supplement 1 (at the back of this report). The general conclusions of the information presented in Supplement 1 include (1) AMLE regression provides the most accurate estimates of censored concentrations for water year 2009 data for the high-intensity stations and 2006–09 data for the low-intensity stations, and (2) differences between results of the AMLE regression method and results of the substitution method generally are relatively small and do not substantially affect comparison of load estimates among water years.

The effect of censored values on statistical analyses generally was minor, with the possible exception of data sets with greater than about 50-percent censored values (table 4; hereinafter referred to as highly censored data sets), and include (1) unfiltered-recoverable cadmium for Blackfoot River near Bonner; (2) unfiltered-recoverable cadmium for Bitterroot near Missoula; and (3) unfiltered-recoverable cadmium, copper, and zinc for Flathead River at Perma. The very large percent (94.4 percent; table 4) of censored values for unfiltered-recoverable cadmium for Flathead River at Perma precluded the use of any

method for estimating censored concentrations and no load estimates are presented in this report for unfiltered-recoverable cadmium for Flathead River at Perma. Statistical relations and load estimates for the highly censored data sets have a greater degree of uncertainty than for other data sets. However, the highly censored data sets still provide useful information for evaluating relative variability in load estimates among sites and years because (1) censored values generally were associated with low to moderate streamflows and did not substantially affect estimates of daily loads during high-flow periods when the largest constituent transport occurs; and (2) variability in trace-element concentrations among samples for the highly censored data sets generally was small, especially for samples collected during low to moderate streamflows. Thus, although the load estimates for the highly censored data sets potentially are subject to greater error, their presentation is warranted to provide an important indication of constituent transport in the Clark Fork basin.

Estimation of Constituent Loads for High-Intensity Stations

Methods used to estimate constituent loads for water year 2009 were similar to those used to estimate constituent loads for water year 2008 (Lambing and Sando, 2009). The consistency in methodology provides a solid basis for comparison of load estimates between these two important years whose high-flow periods occurred after the breach of Milltown Dam.

Table 4. Percentage of samples with censored trace-element concentrations, water years 2004–09.

[Light gray shading indicates some censored values. Dark gray shading indicates greater than 50-percent censored values]

Station number	Station name	Percent of samples with censored concentrations (and total number of samples), for indicated trace element						
		Unfiltered-recoverable cadmium	Unfiltered-recoverable copper	Unfiltered-recoverable iron	Unfiltered-recoverable lead	Unfiltered-recoverable manganese	Unfiltered-recoverable zinc	Unfiltered-recoverable arsenic
12334550	Clark Fork at Turah Bridge, near Bonner, Mont.	1.0 (103)	0.0 (103)	0.0 (103)	0.0 (103)	0.0 (103)	0.0 (103)	0.0 (103)
12334570	Clark Fork Bypass, near Bonner, Mont.	0.0 (38)	0.0 (38)	0.0 (38)	0.0 (38)	0.0 (38)	0.0 (38)	0.0 (38)
12340000	Blackfoot River near Bonner, Mont.	77.4 (93)	26.6 (94)	0.0 (94)	6.4 (94)	0.0 (94)	29.0 (93)	8.5 (94)
12340500	Clark Fork above Missoula, Mont.	1.0 (104)	0.0 (104)	0.0 (104)	0.0 (104)	0.0 (104)	0.0 (104)	0.0 (104)
12352500	Bitterroot River near Missoula, Mont.	70.9 (55)	29.1 (55)	0.0 (55)	1.8 (55)	0.0 (55)	16.7 (54)	0.0 (55)
12354500	Clark Fork at St. Regis, Mont.	5.4 (55)	0.0 (55)	0.0 (55)	0.0 (55)	0.0 (55)	0.0 (55)	0.0 (55)
12388700	Flathead River at Perma, Mont.	94.4 (54)	67.9 (53)	0.0 (54)	7.4 (54)	0.0 (54)	75.4 (53)	0.0 (54)

Suspended Sediment

Daily suspended-sediment loads for water year 2009 were estimated directly for each of the three high-intensity stations (fig. 1) by using high-frequency sampling of the daily sediment monitoring program. The concentration data from the high-frequency samples characterized daily temporal variations needed for developing continuous-concentration curves. Daily mean suspended-sediment concentrations were determined from the continuous-concentration curves according to methods described by Porterfield (1972). The daily mean suspended-sediment concentrations then were multiplied by the daily mean streamflows (and a units-conversion constant) to generate a record of daily suspended-sediment loads.

The daily suspended-sediment loads estimated for stations with daily sediment monitoring did not require development of regression equations that relate suspended-sediment discharges to instantaneous streamflow. However, relations between suspended-sediment discharge and streamflow (sediment-transport relations) were developed to examine patterns that could provide information useful in the development of regression equations for estimating trace-element discharges.

The suspended-sediment concentration for each periodic water-quality sample was converted to an equivalent suspended-sediment discharge, in tons per day, according to the equation:

$$Q_{sed} = C_{sed}QK, \qquad (2)$$

where

Q_{sed} is suspended-sediment discharge, in tons per day;

C_{sed} is suspended-sediment concentration, in milligrams per liter;

Q is streamflow, in cubic feet per second; and

K is a units-conversion constant (0.0027 for concentrations in milligrams per liter) to convert instantaneous suspended-sediment discharge to an equivalent daily suspended-sediment discharge.

After suspended-sediment concentrations were converted to suspended-sediment discharges, the relations between suspended-sediment discharge and streamflow for water years 2008–09 were plotted in conjunction with the data for water years 1985–2007 to visually identify changes in sediment-transport characteristics. Sediment-transport relations (fig. 3) for the three high-intensity stations during water years 2008–09 (predominantly after the breach of Milltown Dam) were compared with pre-breach data from water years 1985–2007 to illustrate changes in sediment transport associated with the dam breach and subsequent channel adjustment. Data for water years 2008–09 were segregated into the rising limb and falling limb of the runoff period of the annual hydrograph to provide more detailed illustration of transport processes associated with the dam breach and subsequent

erosion in response to sediment supply and streamflow conditions. The data for the rising and falling limbs of water years 2008–09 were separately fit with locally weighted scatter plot smoothing (LOWESS) lines (Cleveland and McGill, 1984; Cleveland, 1985) that show the central tendencies of the data distributions over the ranges of streamflows sampled during the two periods. The smooth lines are not regression lines and do not imply statistically significant relations; instead, smooth lines are used as a visual indication of temporal differences in sediment-transport characteristics at each of the three stations. An upward shift in the relation indicates a larger load transported for a given streamflow; a downward shift indicates a smaller load transported for a given streamflow.

During water years 2008–09, sediment-transport relations for Clark Fork at Turah Bridge and Blackfoot River near Bonner, which are upstream from the Milltown Reservoir project area, generally were within the typical spread of data that occurred during water years 1985–2007. For both stations, there was a relatively small upward shift in the relations for the rising limb relative to the falling limb in both water year 2008 and water year 2009. This pattern reflects typical sediment-transport characteristics of natural streams that often exhibit a loop effect of sediment supply such that sediment discharge is greater for a given streamflow when the stream is rising than when it is falling (Colby, 1956).

In contrast to the two stations upstream from the project area, a large shift in the sediment-transport relation was apparent for Clark Fork above Missoula (fig. 3C) during the rising limb of water year 2008 (March 28–May 21, 2008) immediately after the breach of Milltown Dam. During this initial post-breach period, the sediment-transport relation generally was substantially higher than sediment transport for water years 1985–2007, especially at higher streamflows. The upward shift in the sediment-transport relation during the rising limb of water year 2008 presumably resulted from localized inputs of sediment from within the project area, including erosion of coffer dam sediment, reservoir bottom sediment, and sediment from the streambed and banks near the upper end of the former reservoir as the river adjusted to the steeper hydraulic gradient caused by the dam breach. The extent of the upward shift also likely was affected by the magnitude of the annual peak flow, which was relatively large in water year 2008 (112 percent of the long-term mean annual peak flow, table 2). The upward shift in the sediment-transport relation during the water year 2008 rising limb was not sustained, however, as indicated by a large downward shift during the falling limb (May 22–September 30, 2008). The very large downward shift of the sediment-transport relation during the falling limb of the post-breach period probably represented a diminished sediment supply after the erosion and transport of large quantities of sediment from the project area during the rising limb. The relation for the falling limb of water year 2008 diverges from the relation for the rising limb at the higher flows and drops to levels near the lower limits of the range in sediment transport for water years 1985–2007.

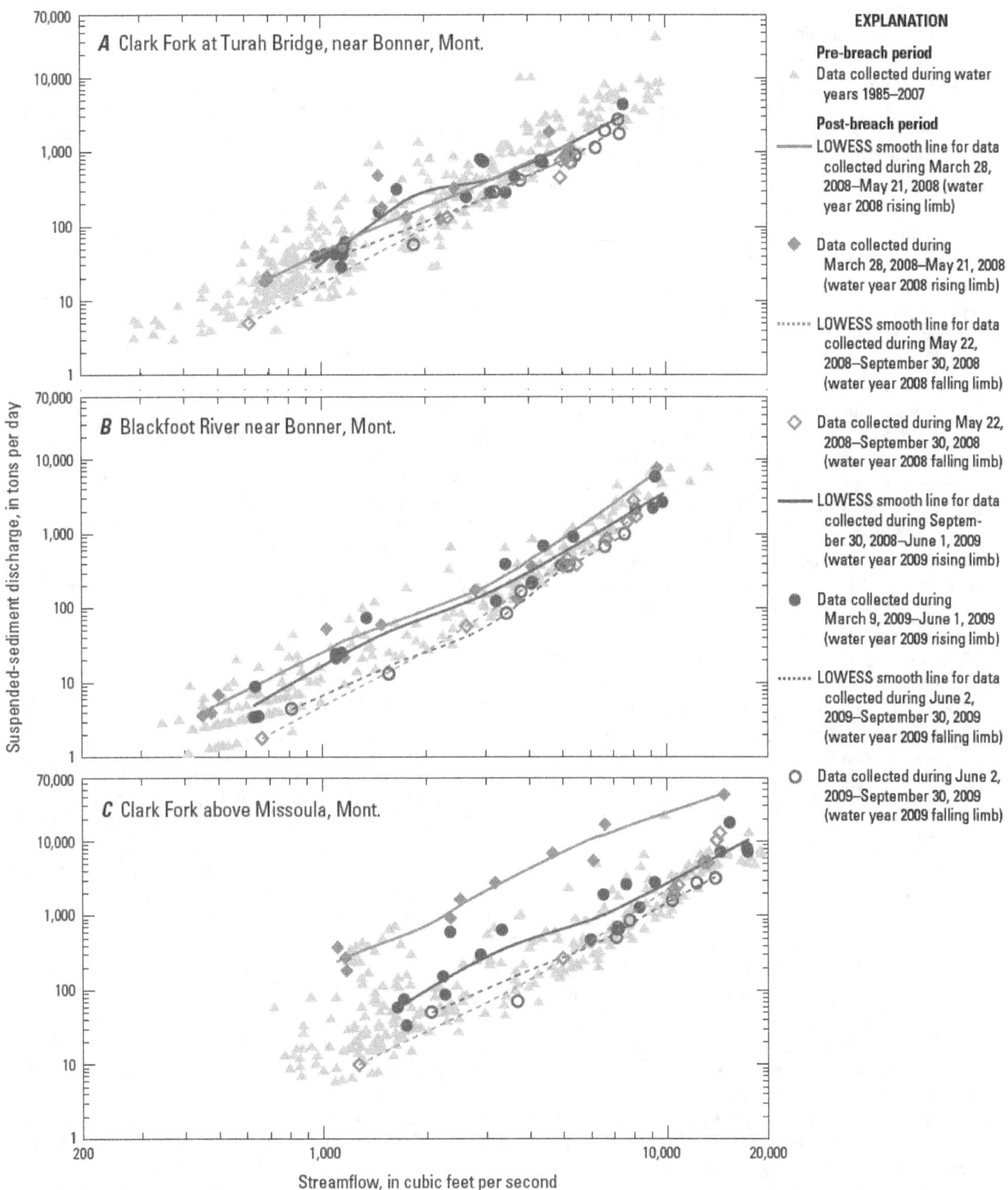

Figure 3. Relations between suspended-sediment discharge and streamflow for water years 2008–09, with comparison to data for water years 1985–2007. *A*, Clark Fork at Turah Bridge, near Bonner, Mont.; *B*, Blackfoot River near Bonner, Mont.; *C*, Clark Fork above Missoula, Mont.

In water year 2009, the sediment-transport relation for the rising limb at the Clark Fork above Missoula generally was substantially below the rising limb for water year 2008, even though streamflows for several samples collected during the rising limb of water year 2009 were substantially larger than those of water year 2008 (fig. 3*C*). The downward shift in the rising-limb relation from water year 2008 to water year 2009 provides further evidence that sediment supply in the project area was substantially depleted by the end of the water year 2008 runoff period. The relatively large variability in sediment transport among individual water samples collected at similar streamflows during the rising limb of water year 2009 probably reflects the erratic streamflow characteristics of the water year 2009 rising limb. During the rising limb of water year 2009, there were several occurrences of sharp rises in streamflow followed by sharp declines in streamflow that were superimposed on the general increase in streamflow (fig. 2). This streamflow pattern in conjunction with typical sediment discharge characteristics (whereby sediment discharge generally is greater for a given streamflow when the stream is rising than when it is falling; Colby, 1956) probably contributed to the large variability in sediment transport at similar stream-flows. The sediment transport measured for many individual water samples collected during the high-flow conditions of the water year 2009 rising limb generally was similar to that of high-flow water samples collected during water years 1985–2007. In water year 2009, there was a downward shift of the falling-limb sediment-transport relation from the rising-limb relation, but the magnitude of the downward shift was substantially smaller in water year 2009 than in water year 2008. The water year 2009 falling-limb sediment-transport relation generally was similar to that of water year 2008 and generally was near the lower limits of the range in sediment transport for water years 1985–2007.

Trace Elements

Daily loads of unfiltered-recoverable trace elements for water year 2009 were estimated for each of the three high-intensity stations (fig. 1) by using regression relations developed from instantaneous streamflow at the time of sampling and concentration data for periodic water-quality samples collected during all or part of water years 2004–09. Data for the entire 6-year period were used to develop trace-element transport relations for water year 2009 at Clark Fork at Turah Bridge and Blackfoot River near Bonner. However, because the remediation activities related to the removal of Milltown Dam resulted in large temporal variability in trace-element transport relations for Clark Fork above Missoula, data used to develop water year 2009 relations were restricted to the period after May 22, 2008 (start of the water year 2008 falling limb of the runoff period). The data were segregated into periods with similar transport relations to develop separate equations for each period, consistent with methods used for estimating loads for water year 2008 (Lambing and Sando, 2009).

Trace-element transport relations (fig. 4) for the three high-intensity stations during water years 2008–09 (after the breach of Milltown Dam) were compared with data for water years 1985–2007 (the entire period of record before 2008) to investigate changes in trace-element transport relations associated with the dam breach and resulting erosion from the project area. Plots for the trace elements cadmium, copper, iron, lead, manganese, and zinc were constructed by using suspended-sediment discharge as the explanatory variable because unfiltered-recoverable concentrations for these trace elements in the Clark Fork basin generally are strongly associated with suspended-sediment concentrations (Lambing, 1991). For example, the median ratio of filtered (representing dissolved phase) to unfiltered copper concentration for water samples collected at Clark Fork above Missoula during water years 1990–2009 is about 0.18; thus, particulate copper concentrations that are associated with suspended sediment typically account for about 82 percent of unfiltered-recoverable copper concentrations. Plots for the metalloid trace element arsenic were constructed by using streamflow as the explanatory variable because concentrations of arsenic in the Clark Fork basin generally are predominantly transported in dissolved phase. For example, the median ratio of filtered to unfiltered arsenic concentration for water samples collected at Clark Fork above Missoula during water years 1990–2009 is about 0.70; thus, filtered (dissolved phase) arsenic concentrations typically account for about 70 percent of unfiltered-recoverable arsenic concentrations and variability in arsenic discharges generally is strongly influenced by variability in streamflow. However, arsenic transport relations in the Clark Fork basin are more complex than the other trace elements. Arsenic particulate concentrations in parts of the Clark Fork basin can be relatively large at times; thus, during periods when there is large suspended-sediment transport, arsenic transport might be predominantly in particulate phase.

The trace-element concentration for each periodic water-quality sample was converted to an equivalent trace-element discharge, in tons per day, according to the equation:

$$Q_{te} = C_{te}QK, \qquad (3)$$

where

Q_{te} is trace-element discharge, in tons per day;
C_{te} is trace-element concentration, in micrograms per liter;
Q is streamflow, in cubic feet per second; and
K is a units-conversion constant (0.0000027 for concentrations in micrograms per liter) to convert instantaneous trace-element discharge to an equivalent daily trace-element discharge.

After trace-element concentrations were converted to trace-element discharges, the relations between trace-element discharge and suspended-sediment discharge or streamflow for water years 2008–09 were plotted in conjunction with the data for water years 1985–2007 to visually identify patterns in trace-element transport characteristics. Data for water years 2008–09 were segregated into the rising limb and falling limb of the runoff period of the annual hydrograph to provide more detailed illustration of trace-element transport processes associated with the dam breach and changes in sediment supply and streamflow conditions. The data for the rising and falling limbs of water years 2008–09 were separately fit with LOWESS smooth lines showing the central tendencies of the data distribution over the range of sediment discharge or streamflows sampled during the two periods. Although smooth plots were examined for all the trace elements, only copper and arsenic are presented as examples (figs. 4 and 5, respectively) because they represent the greatest difference in chemical characteristics and transport relations among the trace elements; the transport relations for the other trace elements generally were similar to those for copper. The smooth lines are not regression lines and do not imply statistically significant relations, but rather are used as a visual indication of temporal differences in trace-element transport characteristics at each of the three high-intensity stations.

During 2008–09, copper- and arsenic-transport relations for Clark Fork at Turah Bridge and Blackfoot River near Bonner, which are upstream from the Milltown Reservoir project area, generally were consistent and within the typical spread of data for water years 1985–2007. As a result of the similarity of temporal patterns indicated by smooth plots for the different periods during water years 2008–09, transport relations for all the trace elements at Clark Fork at Turah Bridge and Blackfoot River near Bonner were considered to be equivalent throughout the entire regression-analysis period (water years 2004–09). Therefore, trace-element discharge for the entire water year 2009 were estimated by single regression equations for each trace element at Clark Fork at Turah Bridge (Supplement 2, table S2.1 at the back of the report) and Blackfoot River near Bonner (Supplement 2, table S2.2). This approach for segregating the data to guide the development of single or multiple regression equations for estimating water year 2009 trace-element loads for these two stations is consistent with the approach used for estimating water year 2008 trace-element loads (Lambing and Sando, 2009).

In contrast to the two high-intensity stations upstream from the project area, an upward shift in the copper- and arsenic-transport relations was apparent for Clark Fork above Missoula (figs. 4C and 5C) during the rising limb of water year 2008 (March 28–May 21, 2008) immediately after the breach of Milltown Dam. The upward shift in the copper-transport relation (based on suspended-sediment discharge) during the water year 2008 rising limb (after the breach of Milltown Dam) presumably was due to increased erosion of copper-enriched sediments that had accumulated in the project area. Examination of the copper content of the suspended sediment (that is, solid-phase concentration) for individual water samples collected before and after the breach of Milltown provides information relevant to the upward shift in the copper. The solid-phase copper concentration was calculated according to the equation:

$$C_{sp} = ((C_{ufr} - C_{fr})/C_{ss}) * 1000, \qquad (4)$$

where

C_{sp} is trace-element solid-phase concentration, in micrograms per gram;

C_{ufr} is trace-element unfiltered-recoverable concentration, in micrograms per liter;

C_{fr} is trace-element filtered-recoverable concentration, in micrograms per liter; and

C_{ss} is suspended-sediment concentration, in milligrams per liter.

The solid-phase copper concentration of the suspended sediment for the periodic water sample collected on March 24, 2008 (immediately before the breach of Milltown Dam), was 152 micrograms per gram (μg/g); the solid-phase copper concentration of the suspended sediment for the sample collected on March 31, 2008 (immediately after the breach of Milltown Dam), was 2,350 μg/g. Thus, there was a large increase in the solid-phase concentration of the suspended sediment for Clark Fork above Missoula immediately after the breach of Milltown Dam that contributed to the upward shift in the copper transport relation (fig. 4C).

There also was a distinct upward shift in the arsenic transport relation (based on streamflow) during the water year 2008 rising limb, primarily due to an associated upward shift in the suspended-sediment transport relation (fig. 3C) and increased erosion of arsenic-enriched sediment that had accumulated in the project area. Based on data collected during water years 1990–2009, filtered (dissolved phase) arsenic concentrations typically (on a median basis) accounted for about 70 percent of unfiltered-recoverable arsenic concentrations and variability in arsenic discharges generally was strongly influenced by variability in streamflow. However, during the water year 2008 rising-limb, arsenic transport at Clark Fork above Missoula was dominated by solid-phase transport due to the large amount of suspended sediment transported from the project area (fig. 3C). During the water year 2008 rising limb, filtered arsenic concentrations typically accounted for about 30 percent of unfiltered-recoverable arsenic concentrations. Thus, solid-phase arsenic concentrations associated with suspended sediment typically accounted for about 70 percent of unfiltered-recoverable arsenic concentrations during the water year 2008 rising limb. During the falling limb of water year 2008 and continuing into water year 2009, the arsenic-transport relation (based on streamflow) generally was consistent and within the typical spread of data for water years 1985–2007.

The water year 2009 data for Clark Fork above Missoula were segregated relative to rising limb and falling limb because (1) there were adequate data in each of the periods to represent the relations during the specific period, and (2) this approach of segregating the data to develop separate regression equations for estimating trace-element loads for different hydrologic periods of water year 2009 for Clark Fork above Missoula is consistent with the approach used for estimating water year 2008 trace-element loads. Using the same

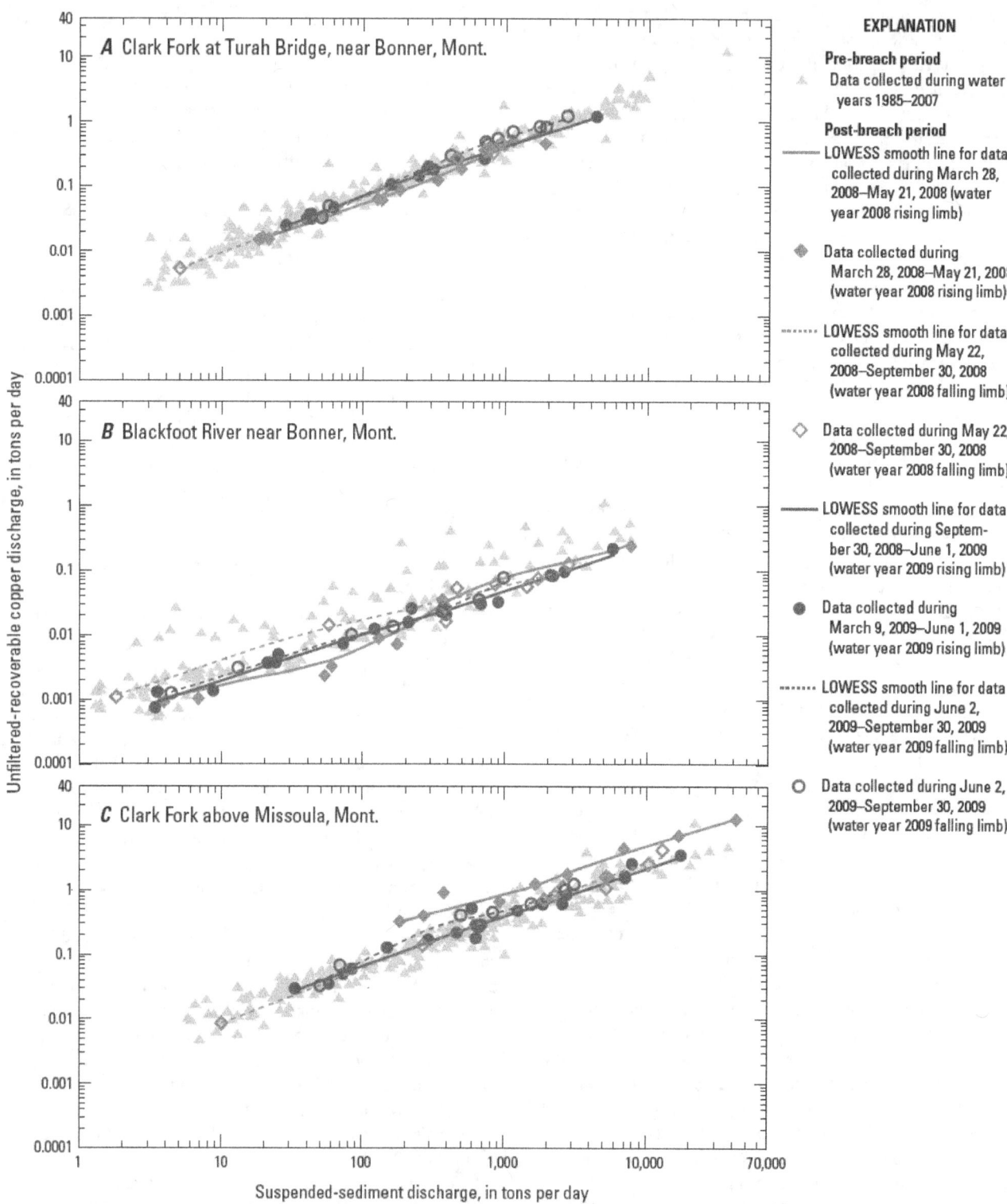

Figure 4.   Relations between unfiltered-recoverable copper discharge and suspended-sediment discharge for water years 2008–09, with comparison to data for water years 1985–2007. *A*, Clark Fork at Turah Bridge, near Bonner, Mont.; *B*, Blackfoot River near Bonner, Mont.; *C*, Clark Fork above Missoula, Mont.

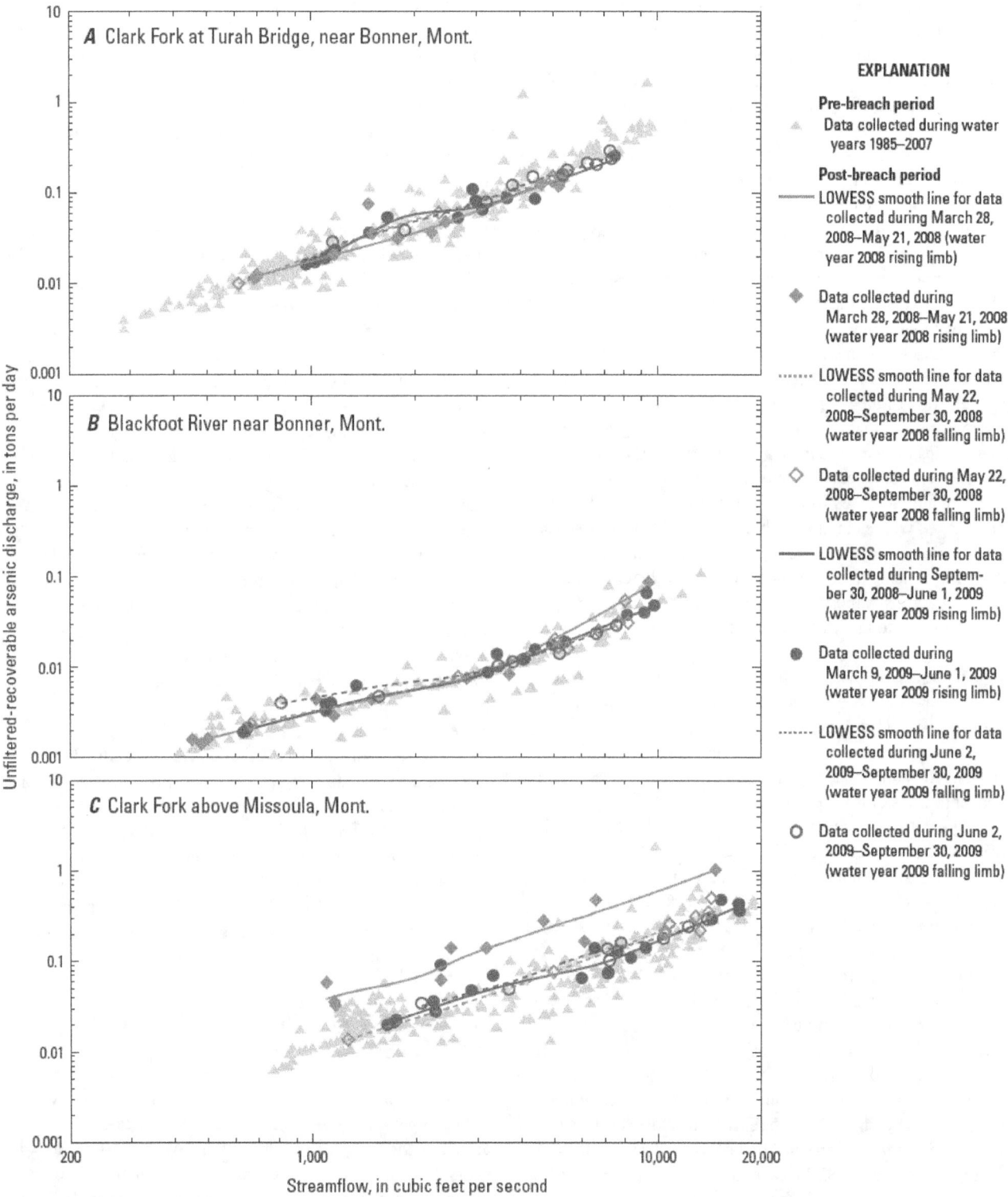

Figure 5. Relations between unfiltered-recoverable arsenic discharge and streamflow for water years 2008–09, with comparison to data for water years 1985–2007. *A*, Clark Fork at Turah Bridge, near Bonner, Mont.; *B*, Blackfoot River near Bonner, Mont.; *C*, Clark Fork above Missoula, Mont.

hydrologically based periods for data segregation ensured a similar treatment of data between water years 2008 and 2009 and provided a consistent approach for comparison of load estimates between these two important years whose high-flow periods occurred after the breach of Milltown Dam.

Although LOWESS smooth lines of trace-element discharge relative to suspended-sediment discharge or streamflow were evaluated to identify temporal patterns useful for guiding data segregation in subsequent regression analysis, regression relations also were more broadly examined. Various combinations of variables, data segregation, and data transformation were tested and regression diagnostics were reviewed to determine the best possible data fit for estimating trace-element discharge. Regression relations between trace-element discharge and the two related variables—streamflow and suspended-sediment discharge—were examined to aid in the selection of the most appropriate explanatory variable in the regression equations. In addition to reviewing regression diagnostics to select the most appropriate explanatory variable, measured instantaneous trace-element discharges for periodic water-quality samples were converted to equivalent daily loads and plotted with estimated daily trace-element loads derived from various forms of regression equations. The estimated daily trace-element loads generated from each combination of data treatments then were compared to measured trace-element loads to identify the form of equation that produced the best matches.

In almost all instances, better relations for estimating water year 2009 trace-element discharge were obtained by using suspended-sediment discharge as the explanatory variable, presumably because of the strong association between suspended-sediment concentrations and unfiltered-recoverable concentrations of trace elements (Lambing, 1991). However, water year 2009 arsenic relations generally were better defined using streamflow as the explanatory variable.

Regression equations for estimating unfiltered-recoverable trace-element discharge for Clark Fork at Turah Bridge, Blackfoot River near Bonner, and Clark Fork above Missoula for water year 2009, and the period of record used to develop the equations, are presented in Supplement 2. As part of regression analysis, the data were transformed to various units and examined to determine which form produced the best linear distribution and fit of a regression line. Values of both trace-element discharge and suspended-sediment discharge were transformed to base 10 logarithm (log) units to obtain the best linear distribution and least scatter for all relations, with the exception of arsenic at Clark Fork at Turah Bridge (Supplement 2, table S2.1), Blackfoot River near Bonner (Supplement 2, table S2.2), and Clark Fork above Missoula (Supplement 2, table S2.2; nonrising-limb periods). In the equations for cadmium, copper, iron, lead, manganese, and zinc, both trace-element discharge and suspended-sediment discharge were transformed to log units, and the equations are presented in exponential form. The equations for estimating unfiltered-recoverable arsenic discharge used streamflow as the explanatory variable, which generally was transformed

to cube root ($Q^{0.333}$) and arsenic discharge was transformed to log units. Single equations describe trace-element discharge for the entire water year 2009 at Clark Fork at Turah Bridge (Supplement 2, table S2.1) and Blackfoot River near Bonner (table Supplement 2, table S2.2). Three separate equations (pre-rising limb, rising limb, and falling limb) describe trace-element discharge for Clark Fork above Missoula (Supplement 2, table S2.3).

All the regression equations for estimating trace-element discharge (Supplement 2) for the high-intensity stations are statistically significant (p-value <0.001). The large R^2 values (average 0.97 and ranging from 0.94 to 1.00) and small SE values (average 22.8 percent and ranging from 11.4 to 36.3 percent) indicate good transport relations for all the trace elements at all three stations. The averages (and ranges) of SE values in the equations for all three stations were 27.3 percent (range 22.3 to 35.1 percent) for cadmium, 26.0 percent (range 18.8 to 36.3 percent) for copper, 18.0 percent (range 11.4 to 26.1 percent) for iron, 26.6 percent (range 21.3 to 34.5 percent) for lead, 18.7 percent (range 16.1 to 24.1 percent) for manganese, 24.8 percent (range 19.8 to 29.5 percent) for zinc, and 18.1 percent (range 13.7 to 25.0 percent) for arsenic. The regression equations in Supplement 2 were applied to the record of either daily mean streamflow or daily suspended-sediment loads to estimate daily trace-element loads for water year 2009. The retransformed results were multiplied by retransformation-bias-correction factors to compensate for log-retransformation bias (Koch and Smillie, 1986) by using procedures described by Duan (1983); retransformation-bias-correction factors ranged from 1.00 to 1.02.

The equations for estimating unfiltered-recoverable trace-element discharge in Supplement 2 describe the relations only for the range of streamflow that was sampled at each station during the period used to develop the equation; therefore, extrapolation to higher streamflows might be subject to substantial error. The separate equations for estimating trace-element discharge at Clark Fork above Missoula are applicable only to the specific dates for the hydrologic periods indicated in table S2.3 of Supplement 2.

Estimation of Constituent Loads for Low-Intensity Stations

Constituent loads for the low-intensity stations have not been previously estimated or reported. Data-collection activities for the low-intensity stations were restricted to water years 2006–09. Further, data collection for the low-intensity stations in each water year was restricted to the seasonal runoff period of the annual hydrograph (generally March–July), with no data collected during extended base-flow conditions.

Annual loads were not estimated for the low-intensity station Clark Fork Bypass near Bonner (station 12334570), which was established within the project area in water year 2008 (table 1 and fig. 1, map number 2) to provide additional spatial resolution on transport characteristics in a reach of channel near the upper end of the former Milltown Reservoir. The Clark Fork Bypass near Bonner has no streamflow-gaging station or daily sediment monitoring, and the channel configuration at the site resulted in irregular flow conditions that complicated the collection of representative isokinetic samples; thus, daily and cumulative loads are not presented for this site. Instead, results for periodic water-quality samples collected on 16 concurrent dates during water year 2008 and 20 concurrent dates during water year 2009 at Clark Fork at Turah Bridge and Clark Fork Bypass near Bonner were compared to evaluate transport characteristics in a reach of channel near the upper end of the former Milltown Reservoir. The two sites are within 5 mi of each other and samples typically were collected within 2–3 hours of each other, which generally corresponded to the travel time through the reach.

For the three low-intensity stations (table 1 and fig. 1, map numbers 5–7) downstream from the project area outflow at Clark Fork above Missoula (table 1 and fig.1, map number 4), data-collection activities did not include high-frequency sampling for daily sediment monitoring; however, all three stations had continuous streamflow-gaging stations. Thus, to estimate suspended-sediment loads, development of regression equations that relate suspended-sediment discharges to instantaneous streamflow (sediment-transport relations) was required. Because all constituent loads (both suspended-sediment and trace-element loads) for the low-intensity stations were estimated using regression methods, discussion of the estimation methods for both suspended sediment and trace elements are included in this single section of this report.

Before developing the regression equations for the low-intensity stations, temporal variability in constituent-transport relations was evaluated using methods similar to those used for the high-intensity stations. Constituent-transport relations for the low-intensity stations are illustrated by scatter plots with LOWESS smooth lines of data for selected constituents for water years 2006–09 (figs. 6–8). Data for the rising limb and falling limb of water years 2008–09 were segregated, and fit with smooth lines to compare pre-breach and post-breach transport patterns and to maintain consistency with data presentation for the high-intensity stations. Although plots were examined for all the trace elements, only copper and arsenic are presented as examples (figs. 7 and 8, respectively). The plots in figures 6–8 serve as examples of the methods and considerations used for segregating the data for regression analyses.

The less intensive data-collection activities for the low-intensity stations complicated regression analyses. Sometimes, transport relations were somewhat to substantially different between the hydrologically based segregation periods, but there were insufficient data to adequately define the relations within a given period. In some cases, this resulted in the need to combine data for the different hydrologic periods to perform regression analysis, which contributed to larger estimation errors and less confidence in the regression equations for the low-intensity stations than for the high-intensity stations. Also, because of the lack of daily suspended-sediment

monitoring at low-intensity stations, streamflow was used as the explanatory variable for all trace-element transport relations. Consequently, the presentation of load estimates for the low-intensity stations is more qualitative, and emphasis generally is placed on relative comparison of results and general transport patterns between stations and between years, rather than on absolute magnitude of load estimates. In conjunction with the limited presentation of results, less detail in discussion of methods is provided for the low-intensity stations than for the high-intensity stations.

Bitterroot River near Missoula represents a major tributary source area that was not influenced by activities related to the removal of Milltown Dam. Constituent-transport relations for Bitterroot River near Missoula for water years 2006–09 were best defined by using separate regression equations for two different periods (Supplement 3, table S3.1 at the back of this report) representing (1) the water years 2006–09 rising limbs of the runoff periods, and (2) the water years 2006–09 falling limbs of the runoff periods (and all other nonrising-limb periods).

Clark Fork at St. Regis is located on the main stem downstream from the project area, resulting in large potential for constituent-transport relations to be strongly influenced by activities related to the removal of Milltown Dam. Constituent-transport relations for Clark Fork at St. Regis for water years 2006–09 were best defined by using separate regression equations for five different periods (Supplement 3, table S3.2) representing (1) the water years 2006–07 rising limbs of the runoff periods, (2) the water years 2006–07 falling limbs of the runoff periods (and all other nonrising-limb periods), (3) the water year 2008 rising limb of the runoff period, (4) the water year 2009 rising limb of the runoff period, and (5) the water years 2008–09 falling limbs of the runoff periods (and all other nonrising-limb periods).

Flathead River at Perma represents a major tributary source area that was not influenced by activities related to the removal of Milltown Dam. Constituent-transport relations for Flathead River at Perma for water years 2006–09 were best defined by using separate regression equations for three different periods (Supplement 3, table S3.3) representing (1) the water years 2006–07 and water year 2009 rising limbs of the runoff periods, (2) the water year 2008 rising limb of the runoff period, and (3) the water years 2006–09 falling limbs of the runoff periods (and all other nonrising-limb periods).

Regression equations (and associated information) for estimating constituent loads for water years 2006–09 at Bitterroot River near Missoula, Clark Fork at St. Regis, and Flathead River at Perma are presented in Supplement 3. As part of regression analysis, the data were transformed to various units and examined to determine which form produced the best linear distribution and fit of a regression line. Values for constituent discharge were transformed to log units and streamflow values were transformed to either log units, square roots ($Q^{0.500}$), or cube roots ($Q^{0.333}$) to obtain the best linear distribution and least scatter. The equations apply only to the dates for the individual hydrologic periods indicated in Supplement 3.

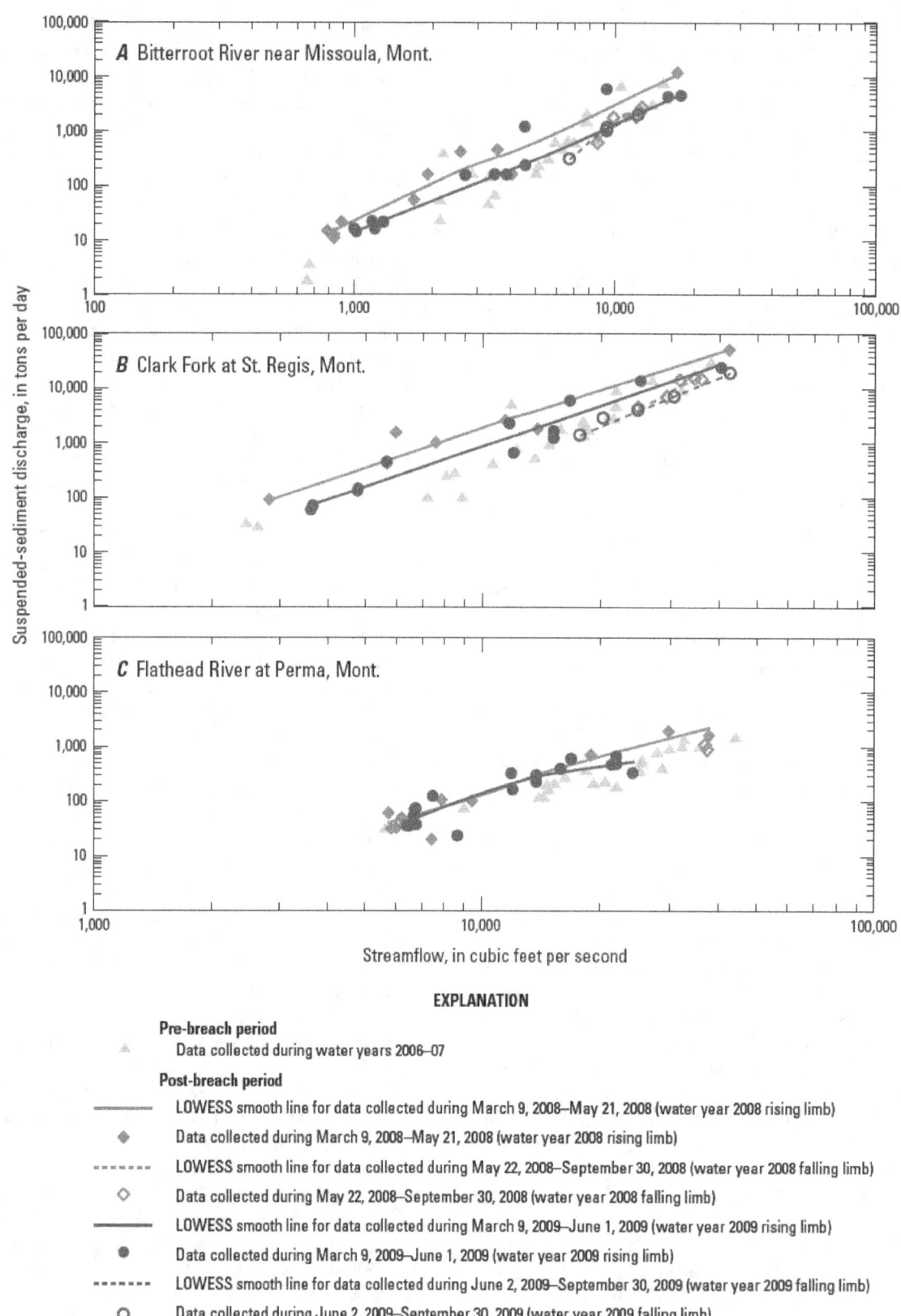

Figure 6.   Relations between suspended-sediment discharge and streamflow for water years 2008–09, with comparison to data for water years 2006–07. *A*, Bitterroot River near Missoula, Mont.; *B*, Clark Fork at St. Regis, Mont.; *C*, Flathead River at Perma, Mont.

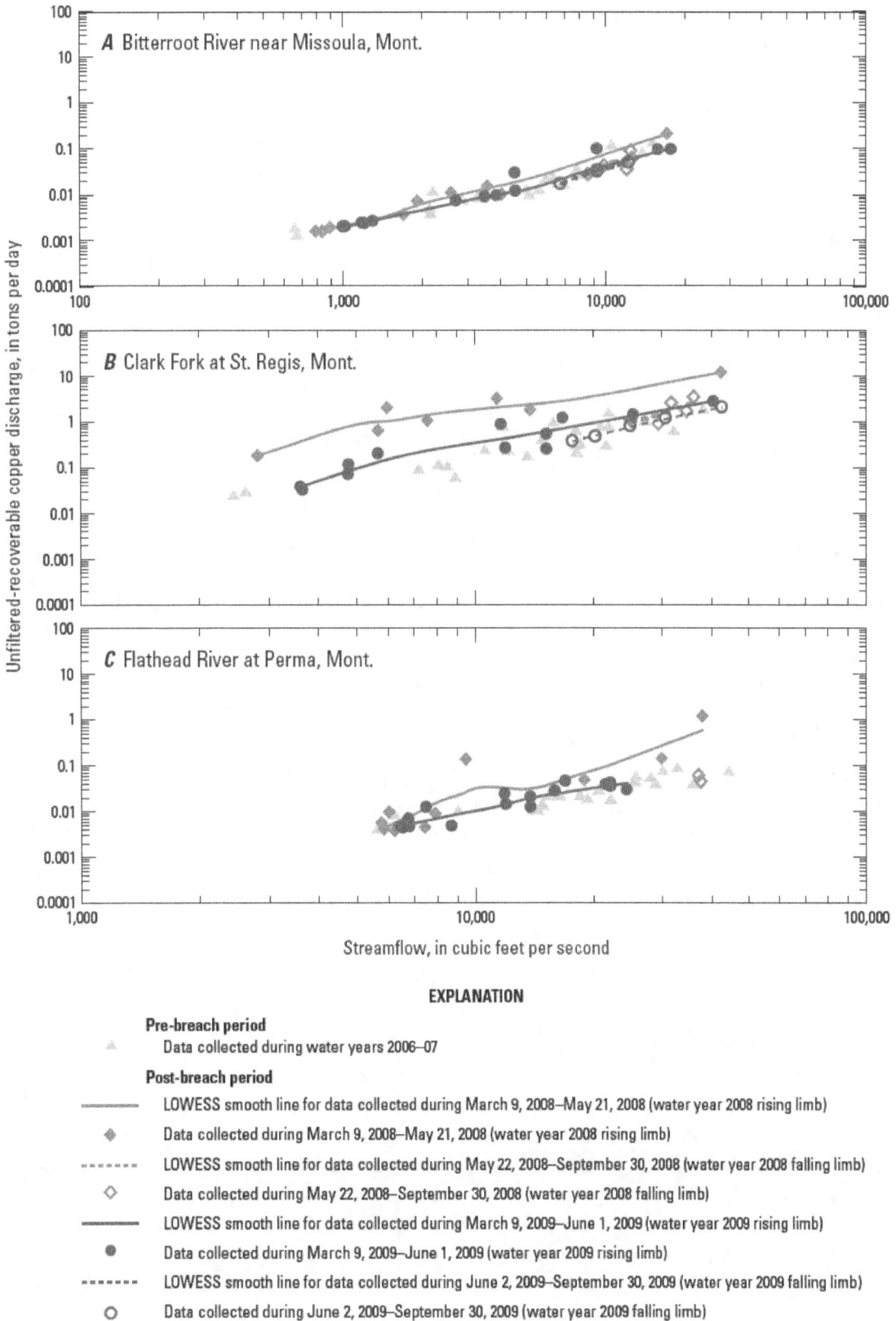

Figure 7. Relations between unfiltered-recoverable copper discharge and streamflow for water years 2008–09, with comparison to data for water years 2006–07. *A*, Bitterroot River near Missoula, Mont.; *B*, Clark Fork at St. Regis, Mont.; *C*, Flathead River at Perma, Mont.

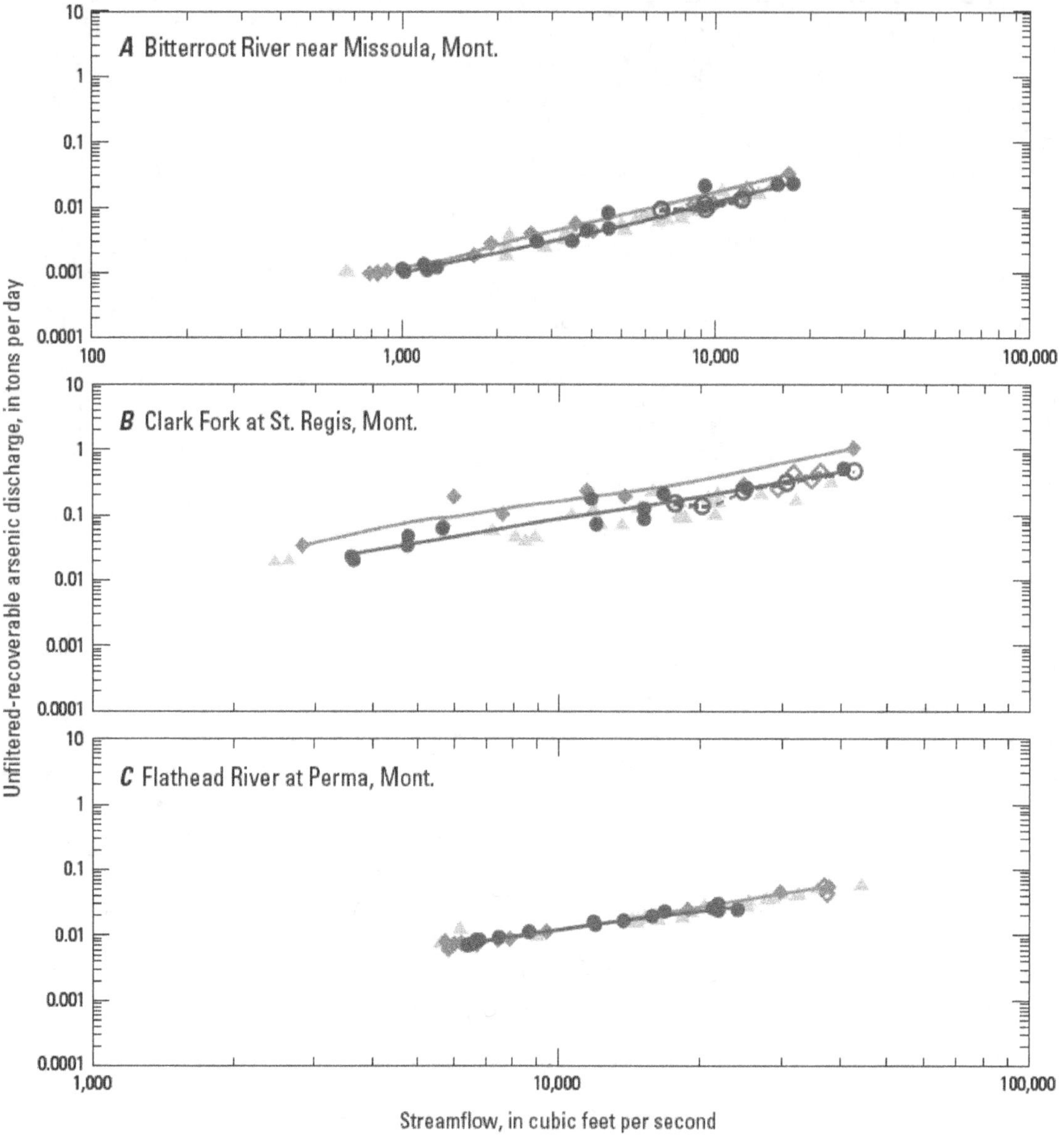

EXPLANATION

Pre-breach period

▲ Data collected during water years 2006–07

Post-breach period

───── LOWESS smooth line for data collected during March 9, 2008–May 21, 2008 (water year 2008 rising limb)

◆ Data collected during March 9, 2008–May 21, 2008 (water year 2008 rising limb)

------ LOWESS smooth line for data collected during May 22, 2008–September 30, 2008 (water year 2008 falling limb)

◇ Data collected during May 22, 2008–September 30, 2008 (water year 2008 falling limb)

───── LOWESS smooth line for data collected during March 9, 2009–June 1, 2009 (water year 2009 rising limb)

● Data collected during March 9, 2009–June 1, 2009 (water year 2009 rising limb)

------ LOWESS smooth line for data collected during June 2, 2009–September 30, 2009 (water year 2009 falling limb)

○ Data collected during June 2, 2009–September 30, 2009 (water year 2009 falling limb)

Figure 8. Relations between unfiltered-recoverable arsenic discharge and streamflow for water years 2008–09, with comparison to data for water years 2006–07. *A*, Bitterroot River near Missoula, Mont.; *B*, Clark Fork at St. Regis, Mont.; *C*, Flathead River at Perma, Mont.

All the regression equations for estimating suspended-sediment discharge (Supplement 3) for the low-intensity stations are statistically significant (p-values <0.001). The relatively large R^2 values (average 0.92 and ranging from 0.81 to 0.98) and generally moderate SE values (average 46.7 percent and ranging from 17.6 to 76.1 percent) indicate reasonably accurate transport relations for the low-intensity stations. The SE values for the suspended-sediment equations generally were less than or similar to SE values for suspended-sediment equations previously used to estimate suspended-sediment loads in the Clark Fork basin (Lambing, 1991; Hornberger and others, 1997; Lambing, 1998; Lambing and Sando, 2008, 2009). However, there is substantially lower confidence in the suspended-sediment load estimates for the low-intensity stations that are based on regressions with streamflow than for the high-intensity stations that are determined from high-frequency daily sediment monitoring.

All the regression equations for estimating trace-element discharge (Supplement 3) for the low-intensity stations are statistically significant (p-values ranging <0.001 to 0.003). The generally moderate R^2 values (average 0.88 and ranging from 0.40 to 0.99) and generally moderate SE values (average 39.1 percent and ranging from 7.6 to 101.1 percent) indicate reasonably accurate transport relations for the low-intensity stations. The SE values for the trace-element equations generally were less than or similar to SE values for trace-element equations previously used to estimate trace-element loads in the Clark Fork basin at stations with similar levels of data collection (Lambing, 1991; Hornberger and others, 1997; Lambing, 1998). The averages (and ranges) of SE values in the equations for all of the low-intensity stations were 41.6 percent (range 19.1 to 63.1 percent) for cadmium, 45.9 percent (range 18.4 to 101.1 percent) for copper, 38.8 percent (range 11.1 to 74.0 percent) for iron, 44.0 percent (range 16.4 to 71.3 percent) for lead, 36.5 percent (range 13.6 to 69.3 percent) for manganese, 45.9 percent (range 22.1 to 69.6 percent) for zinc, and 21.4 percent (range 7.6 to 37.9 percent) for arsenic. The SEs of the trace-element equations for the low-intensity stations generally are substantially larger than for the high-intensity stations and indicate lower confidence in the trace-element load estimates for the low-intensity stations (that are based only on regressions with streamflow) than for the high-intensity stations (that are based on best-fit regressions with either streamflow or suspended-sediment discharge).

The regression equations in Supplement 3 were applied to the record of daily mean streamflow to estimate daily constituent loads for water years 2006–09. The retransformed results were multiplied by retransformation-bias-correction factors to compensate for log-retransformation bias by using procedures described by Duan (1983); retransformation-bias-correction factors ranged from 1.00 to 1.07.

Estimated Loads Transported Through the Milltown Reservoir Project Area

Variability in daily loads transported past the three high-intensity stations that bracket the project area illustrate the response of constituent transport to streamflow variations, ice conditions, reservoir operations, dam-removal activities, and discrete erosional events. Daily loads can be summed for individual periods to determine cumulative loads transported over prolonged periods to indicate the most important source areas contributing constituents to the river on a sustained basis. The cumulative net gains or losses for the periods before and after the breach of Milltown Dam can identify differences in the mass balance for distinctly different environmental settings and flow conditions. Also, the cumulative net gains or losses during a given year can be used to describe the annual mass balance of the suspended-sediment and trace-element loads transported through the project area. Load estimates for the three stations and mass balance of suspended sediment and trace elements within the project area for water year 2009 are presented with comparisons to estimated loads and mass balance within the project area for (1) water years 1985–2005 (average annual load and mass-balance values for all years combined, representing typical conditions during the period before the start of permanent drawdown of Milltown Reservoir on June 1, 2006); (2) water years 1996–97 (average annual load and mass-balance values for both years combined, representing high-flow conditions during the period before the start of permanent drawdown); (3) water years 2006–07 (representing the period between the start of permanent drawdown of Milltown Reservoir and the breach of Milltown Dam); and (4) water year 2008, during which Milltown Dam was breached.

Daily Loads

Variations of estimated daily suspended-sediment, unfiltered-recoverable copper, and unfiltered-recoverable arsenic loads transported as inflow to and outflow from the project area during water years 2004–09 are shown in figures 9–11, respectively, along with the daily mean streamflow during the years. Water years 2004–09 are specifically presented in figures 9–11 to illustrate variability in constituent transport before the start of permanent drawdown, during permanent drawdown, on the day Milltown Dam was breached, and after the breach of Milltown Dam. Daily constituent loads during water years 2004–07 and water year 2008 were previously reported and discussed in detail in Lambing and Sando (2008, 2009). Thus, in this report, variations in constituent loads for water years 2004–08 are briefly summarized and compared with variations for water year 2009, which are discussed in detail.

In figures 9–11, daily values for the two streamflow-gaging stations upstream from the project area (Clark Fork at Turah Bridge and Blackfoot River near Bonner) are summed to represent the total inflow of streamflow and constituent loads from the upstream source areas to the project area. Values determined for Clark Fork at Turah Bridge represent the inflow from the upper Clark Fork basin; values determined for Blackfoot River near Bonner represent the inflow from the Blackfoot River basin. The daily values for Clark Fork above Missoula represent the outflow from the project area. Also shown are measured values of instantaneous constituent discharge (converted to equivalent daily loads by assuming the instantaneous discharge is maintained for 24 hours) for the periodic water-quality samples collected during water years 2004–09 for comparison to the estimated daily loads.

Deposition of constituent load (net gain) within the project area is indicated by black shading of the area between inflow and outflow loads in figures 9–11 for days when the combined inflow load to the project area was greater than the outflow load at Clark Fork above Missoula. Conversely, loss of load (net loss) from the project area is indicated by red shading of the area between inflow and outflow loads for days when the outflow load at Clark Fork above Missoula was greater than the combined inflow load. Differences in daily loads transported to and from the project area illustrate discrete periods of net balance, deposition, or loss of constituent load within the project area. Generally, deposition of sediment and sediment-associated trace elements within the project area is more likely to occur during low streamflows when velocities are low. Loss of sediment and sediment-associated trace elements is more likely to occur during high streamflows when velocities are high; however, deposition or loss of constituents also can result from discrete events or localized activities not directly related to streamflow magnitude.

The gray-shaded area in figures 9–11 represents water years 2004–05 plus the first 7 months of water year 2006 before the start of permanent drawdown of Milltown Reservoir on June 1, 2006. The yellow-shaded area represents the period between the start of permanent drawdown and the breach of Milltown Dam on March 28, 2008. The pink-shaded area represents the period after the breach of Milltown Dam when the environment of the project area changed from a reservoir to a free-flowing river. The color-shading representation of time periods shown in figures 9–11 also is used in other figures in this report. The Y-axes of figures 9–11 are plotted on log scale; thus, the visual appearance of smaller net gains or losses is exaggerated relative to larger net gains or losses.

The annual variability in daily streamflow (figs. 2, 9–11) illustrates a typical snowmelt-dominated hydrograph in which streamflow generally was low to moderate during the fall and winter, then increased for several months during spring runoff, which often starts in early March. During water years 2004–09, streamflow commonly peaked in May or early

June and then decreased to low-flow conditions in late summer. Minimum streamflows often occurred during December or January when base-flow conditions occurred and ice formation further reduced streamflow. Short-lived precipitation events or periods of ice-melt sometimes produced substantial increases in streamflow during general base-flow periods, as evidenced by relatively large increases in streamflow during January 2005, November 2006, November 2008, and January 2009. Differences in daily streamflow between the combined inflow to the project area and the outflow at Clark Fork above Missoula were small. Minor differences between combined inflow and outflow could represent inputs from ungaged small tributaries in the reaches between the streamflow-gaging stations, loss of surface water to groundwater in the alluvium underlying the project area, possible small amounts of evaporative loss from the reservoir surface, or minor inaccuracies in streamflow records.

A detailed description of streamflow conditions during water year 2009 (with comparison to water year 2008) is presented in the section of this report titled "Hydrologic Characteristics." In general, streamflow conditions during water year 2009 were above normal to near normal. Water year 2009 streamflow was especially high during the rising limb of the runoff period, and generally was higher and sustained for a longer time than water year 2008 rising-limb streamflow, although annual peak streamflows were the same for both years.

Suspended Sediment

Variations in estimated daily suspended-sediment loads (fig. 9) transported to and from the project area during the period before the start of permanent drawdown (October 1, 2003–May 31, 2006; fig. 9) generally coincided with variations in streamflow. For most of the period, streamflows were below or near normal (fig. 2) and differences between the daily suspended-sediment loads transported to and from the project area generally were minor (indicating approximate net balance) or indicated small amounts of deposition or scour. However, the outflow of suspended sediment from the project area was substantially greater than the combined inflow during the temporary drawdowns in July–August 2004 and October–December 2005. The increase in suspended-sediment load transported from the project area during the temporary drawdowns occurred during low-flow conditions. Thus, these losses might have resulted from erosion of exposed shoreline sediments or localized disturbances, rather than scour of deeper bottom sediments (Lambing and Sando, 2008).

Consistent net loss of suspended sediment from the project area began with the start of permanent drawdown on June 1, 2006, and continued through the end of the drawdown period marked by the breach of Milltown Dam on March 28, 2008. During the permanent drawdown period, streamflow generally was below normal (fig. 2, table 2), but the pattern of near continuous net loss of suspended sediment persisted for all streamflow conditions and, at times, the loss of sediment

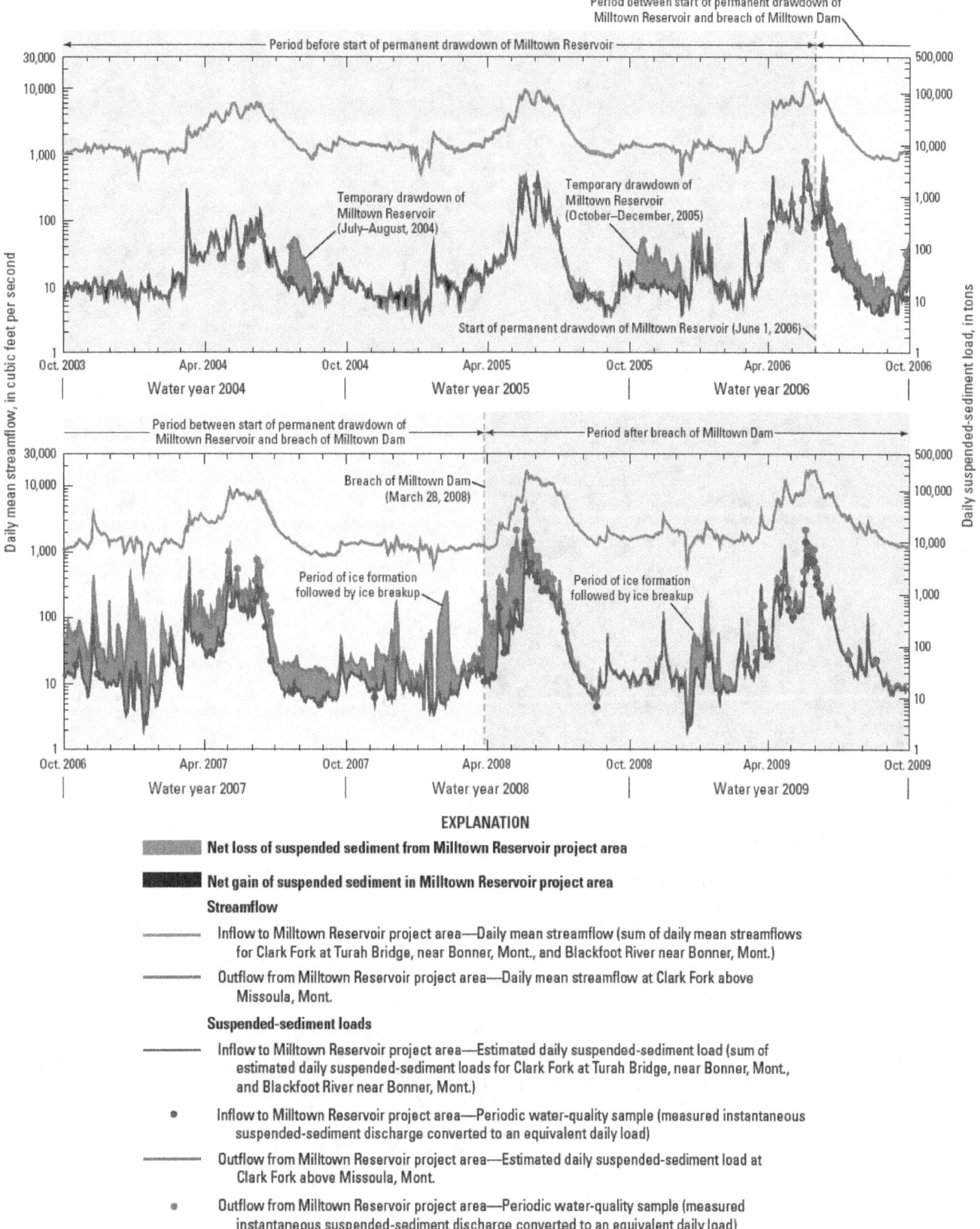

Figure 9.   Daily mean streamflow and estimated daily suspended-sediment loads transported to and from the Milltown Reservoir project area, water years 2004–09.

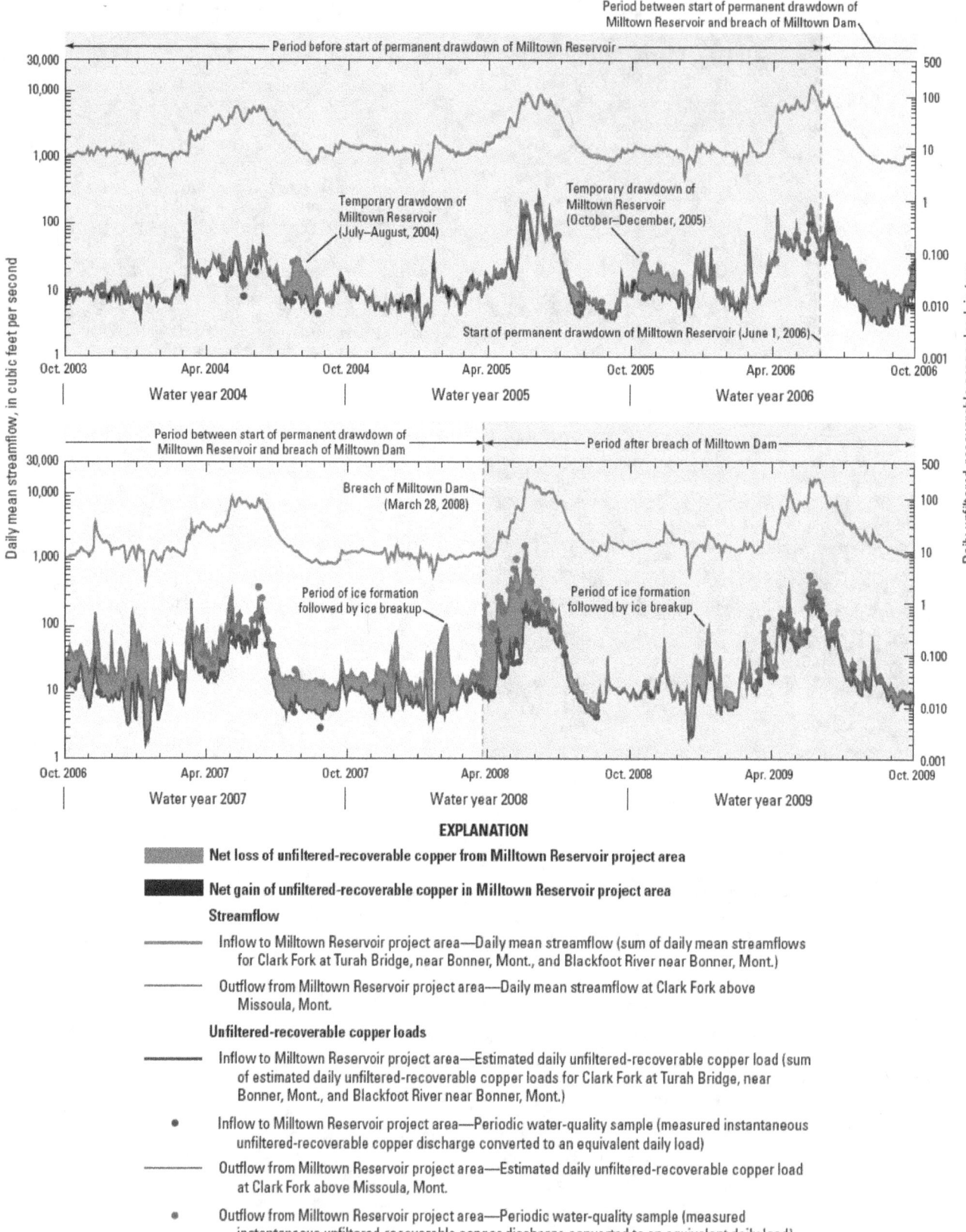

Figure 10.   Daily mean streamflow and estimated daily unfiltered-recoverable copper loads transported to and from the Milltown Reservoir project area, water years 2004–09.

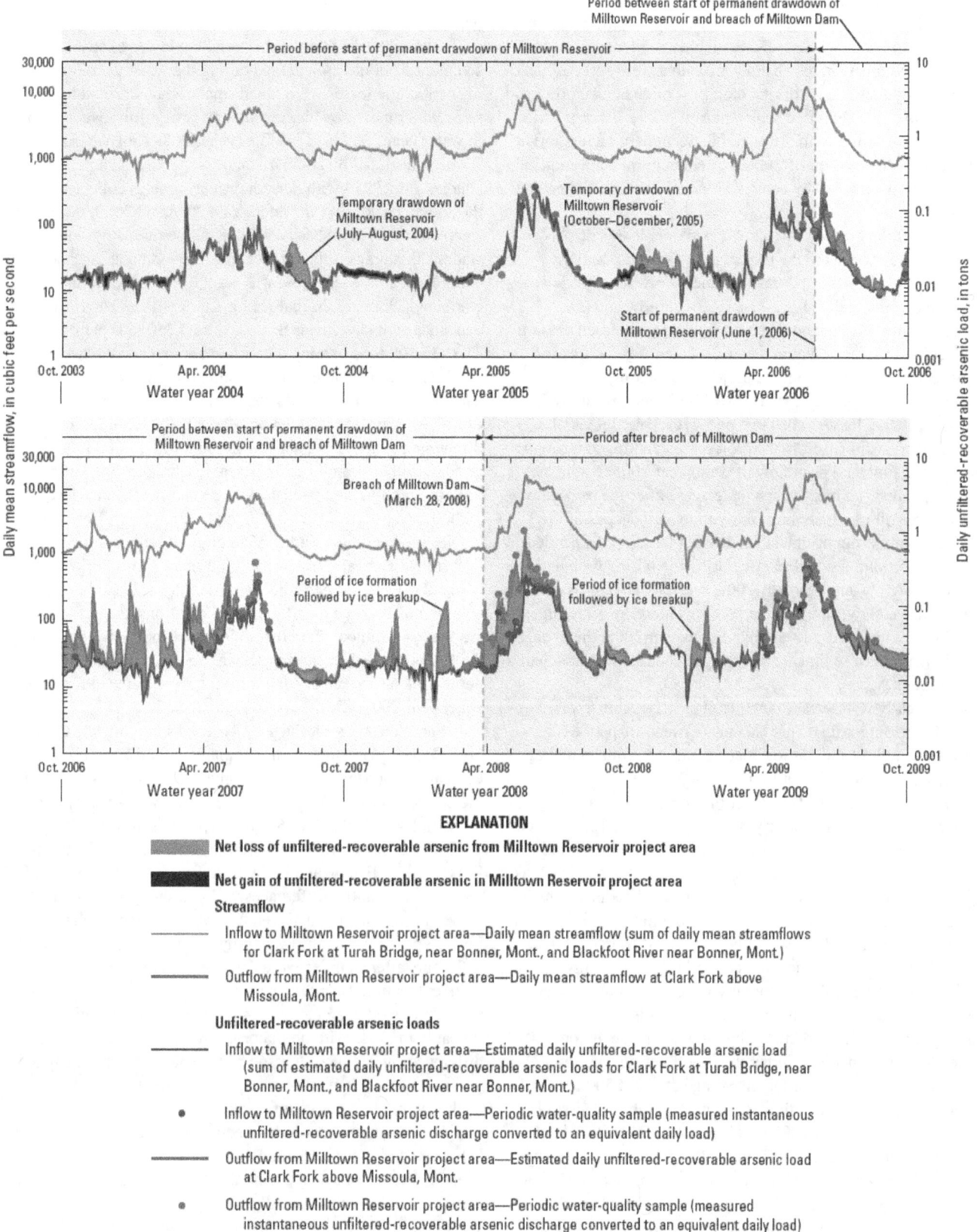

Figure 11.   Daily mean streamflow and estimated daily unfiltered-recoverable arsenic loads transported to and from the Milltown Reservoir project area, water years 2004–09.

from the project area was substantial. The sediment losses from the project area likely were caused by a combination of factors. Primary processes likely included either erosion of bottom sediments in the shallow areas that were susceptible to velocity-induced scour during high flow or channel cutting and bank collapse of exposed sediment as water levels dropped and water drained from the material. Secondary factors might have included erosion of shoreline sediment by wind-induced waves or disturbance by construction activities (Lambing and Sando, 2008).

After the breach of Milltown Dam, net losses of suspended sediment from the project area were substantially greater than those during the permanent drawdown period because of generally above-normal streamflow and the steeper channel gradient that contributed to increased erosion of sediment sources within the project area. The outflow of suspended sediment from the project area sharply increased immediately after the breach of Milltown Dam, resulting in large daily net losses. The large post-breach net losses of suspended sediment from the project area continued through the rising limb and peak flow of water year 2008. Net losses of suspended sediment began to decrease after the peak flow, but were still relatively large during the early stages of the falling limb through June 2008. The net losses of suspended sediment continued to decrease during the falling limb and were relatively small by July 2008, reaching an approximate net balance between inflow and outflow loads by mid-August 2008. From mid-August through September 2008, the average daily net loss of sediment from the project area was less than 1 ton per day.

In early water year 2009 (October 1–December 15, 2008), the approximate net balance between suspended-sediment inflow and outflow loads continued with an average daily net loss of sediment from the project area of less than 5 tons per day. In mid-December through late January, ice conditions caused a relatively large increase in net losses from the project area; the cumulative net loss during this period was about 5,100 tons of sediment for an average of about 113 tons per day. After this erosional event, suspended-sediment net losses decreased to about net balance conditions until the start of the rising limb of the runoff period in mid-March. During the water year 2009 runoff period (about March 9–July 27, 2009) when streamflows generally were above normal, net losses increased substantially (although this is not readily apparent in figure 9 due to the log-scale presentation); the cumulative net loss during the runoff period was about 70,500 tons of sediment for an average of about 500 tons per day. Average streamflow for Clark Fork above Missoula during the water year 2009 runoff period was 6,400 ft³/s. In comparison, during the water year 2008 runoff period (about March 9–August 10, 2008), the cumulative net loss was about 375,000 tons of sediment for an average of about 2,420 tons per day, and the average streamflow at Clark Fork above Missoula was about 5,430 ft³/s. After the water year 2009 runoff period, net losses decreased to about net balance conditions until the end of water year 2009. During the post-runoff period

of water year 2009, the average daily net loss was about 6 tons per day.

Although there were substantial net losses of suspended sediment from the project area during the water year 2009 runoff period, the losses were much smaller than during the water year 2008 runoff period, even though streamflows were higher in water year 2009 than in water year 2008. This pattern is further illustrated by comparison of suspended-sediment discharges associated with periodic water samples collected near the annual peak flows in water years 2008 and 2009. For water samples collected on May 19, 2008, at the three high-intensity stations that bracket the project area, the sediment discharge at Clark Fork above Missoula was 42,400 tons per day, and the combined sediment discharges for Clark Fork at Turah Bridge and Blackfoot River near Bonner were 9,550 tons per day. The –32,800 tons per day net difference (net loss) between the combined inflow and outflow sediment discharges occurred at a streamflow of 14,800 ft³/s for Clark Fork above Missoula. For water samples collected on May 20, 2009, the sediment discharge at Clark Fork above Missoula was 17,500 tons per day, and the combined sediment discharges for Clark Fork at Turah Bridge and Blackfoot River near Bonner were 10,000 tons per day. The -7,500 tons per day net difference between the combined inflow and outflow sediment discharges occurred at a streamflow of 15,400 ft³/s for Clark Fork above Missoula. Thus, for periodic water samples collected during similar streamflow magnitudes and conditions, the net loss of suspended sediment from the project area for the water year 2009 near-peak-flow sample set was about 23 percent of the net loss of suspended sediment from the project area for the water year 2008 near-peak-flow sample set.

Sample results for the supplemental sampling site Clark Fork Bypass near Bonner (fig. 1, map number 2) are useful for evaluating contributions from localized areas of erosion within the project area. A comparison of periodic water-quality data for samples collected on 16 concurrent dates during water year 2008 and 20 concurrent dates during water year 2009 at Clark Fork at Turah Bridge and Clark Fork Bypass near Bonner indicates substantial differences within a short distance (about 5 river mi) of channel between the two sites. Samples at Clark Fork Bypass near Bonner generally were collected within 2 to 3 hours after samples were collected at Clark Fork at Turah Bridge; this time interval approximated the stream travel time, which provided characterization of the same hydrologic condition at both sites. With no major inflows between the two sites, differences in sediment transport presumably can be attributed to erosion from channel sources, such as the streambed and banks, within the intervening reach.

Differences in suspended-sediment concentrations between Clark Fork at Turah Bridge and Clark Fork Bypass near Bonner indicate a substantial input of sediment from the intervening channel, especially during high-flow conditions. The post-breach median suspended-sediment concentration in water year 2008 increased from 39 mg/L at Clark Fork at Turah Bridge to 161 mg/L at Clark Fork Bypass near Bonner for the 16 samples collected on concurrent dates during the runoff period. In water year 2009, the median suspended-sediment concentration increased from 42 mg/L at Clark Fork at Turah Bridge to 78 mg/L at Clark Fork Bypass near Bonner for the 20 samples collected on concurrent dates during the runoff period. Thus, the water year 2009 increase in median suspended-sediment concentration between the two sites was substantially less than the water year 2008 increase, even though water year 2009 streamflows were higher than water year 2008 streamflows. These patterns indicate substantial depletion of readily erodible sediment for the evaluated streamflows in the reach between Clark Fork at Turah Bridge and Clark Fork Bypass near Bonner by the end of water year 2008.

Comparisons between particle-size distributions of suspended sediment at Clark Fork at Turah Bridge and Clark Fork Bypass near Bonner also provide information on differences in sediment composition and transport characteristics between the two sites during water years 2008 and 2009. The post-breach water year 2008 median percent of suspended sediment finer than 0.062 mm (hereinafter referred to as fines) for the concurrent sample sets decreased from 72 percent at Clark Fork at Turah Bridge to 28 percent at Clark Fork Bypass near Bonner. In water year 2009, the median percent fines for the concurrent sample sets decreased from 70 percent at Clark Fork at Turah Bridge to 52 percent at Clark Fork Bypass near Bonner. Thus, there was substantially more sand content in the suspended sediment at Clark Fork Bypass near Bonner than at Clark Fork at Turah Bridge during both water years 2008 and 2009, but the increase in sand content at Clark Fork Bypass near Bonner was less in water year 2009 than in water year 2008.

In both water years 2008 and 2009, the greatest inputs of suspended sediment from the intervening reach between Clark Fork at Turah Bridge and Clark Fork Bypass near Bonner occurred during the rising limb of the runoff period near the annual peaks. For example, the sample of May 19, 2008, at Clark Fork at Turah Bridge had a suspended-sediment concentration of 151 mg/L, with a size composition of 63-percent fines, indicating a predominance of fine sediment. In contrast, the sample collected about 2 hours later at Clark Fork Bypass near Bonner had a suspended-sediment concentration of 3,780 mg/L (a 25-fold increase in concentration in the relatively short intervening reach) and was predominantly sand, with a size composition of 9-percent fines. Near the annual peak in water year 2009, the sample of May 26, 2009, at Clark Fork at Turah Bridge had a suspended-sediment concentration of 136 mg/L, with a size composition of 65-percent fines, indicating predominantly fine sediment. In contrast, the sample collected 2 hours later at Clark Fork Bypass near Bonner had a suspended-sediment concentration of 227 mg/L (a relatively small 1.7-fold increase in concentration in the intervening reach) and had a size composition of 51-percent fines. Although the sand content increased in the intervening reach in water year 2009, the increase was much less than in water year 2008 under similar hydrologic conditions.

The substantial increase during water year 2008 in suspended-sediment concentration and percentage of sand contributed from the short reach between Clark Fork at Turah Bridge and Clark Fork Bypass near Bonner clearly indicates the dynamic process of post-breach channel erosion that occurred during high flow in the area near the upper end of the Clark Fork arm of the former reservoir. The substantially smaller differences during water year 2009 between suspended-sediment concentration and percentage of sand contributed from the short reach between Clark Fork at Turah Bridge and Clark Fork Bypass near Bonner further indicates that there was substantial depletion of erodible channel materials or, possibly greater geomorphic stability, in the reach by the end of water year 2008.

Trace Elements

The temporal variations in daily loads for all the unfiltered-recoverable trace elements (cadmium, copper, iron, lead, manganese, zinc, and arsenic) estimated for water years 2004–09 generally were similar. Estimated daily loads of copper (fig. 10) and arsenic (fig. 11) are illustrated as representative examples of trace-element transport to and from the project area during water years 2004–09. These two elements are presented as examples because they are constituents of concern in terms of potential toxicity and they represent the greatest difference in chemical characteristics and transport relations among the trace elements

Variations in daily copper and arsenic loads entering and leaving the project area generally coincided with variations in streamflow (figs. 10 and 11) and suspended-sediment loads (fig. 9); the daily loads for the other trace elements similarly coincided with variations in streamflow and suspended-sediment loads. The specific temporal variability in daily suspended-sediment loads and associated causal factors previously noted in this report generally apply to variability in daily trace-element loads. However, specific observations concerning daily copper and arsenic loads during high-transport periods in water year 2009 and differences in daily trace-element loads between water year 2008 and water year 2009 are presented to further characterize transport processes.

In early water year 2009 (October 1–December 15, 2008), there was an approximate net balance between copper inflow and outflow loads within the project area, with an average daily net loss of about 0.001 ton per day. During the period of ice conditions in mid-December 2008 through late January 2009, the cumulative net loss of copper from the project area was about 2.47 tons for an average of about 0.055 ton per day. After this erosional event, copper net losses decreased to about net balance conditions until the start of the runoff period in mid-March. During the water year 2009 runoff period (about March 9–July 27, 2009), net losses increased substantially; the cumulative net loss during the runoff period was about 25.5 tons of copper (average of about 0.181 ton per day). Average streamflow for Clark Fork above Missoula during the water year 2009 runoff period was 6,400 ft³/s. In comparison, during the water year 2008 runoff period (about March 9–August 10, 2008), which included the initial post-breach period, the cumulative net loss was about 150 tons of copper (average of about 0.971 ton per day), and the average streamflow at Clark Fork above Missoula was about 5,430 ft³/s. After the water year 2009 runoff period, net losses persisted, but decreased until the end of water year 2009. During the post-runoff period, the average daily net loss was about 0.012 ton per day.

Although there were substantial net losses of copper from the project area during the water year 2009 runoff period, the losses were much smaller than during the water year 2008 runoff period, even though streamflows were higher in water year 2009 than in water year 2008. This pattern is further illustrated by comparison of copper discharges associated with periodic water samples collected near the peak annual flows in water years 2008 and 2009. For water samples collected on May 19, 2008, at the three high-intensity stations that bracket the project area, the copper discharge at Clark Fork above Missoula was 12.3 tons per day, and the combined copper discharges for Clark Fork at Turah Bridge and Blackfoot River near Bonner were 0.704 ton per day. The –11.6 tons per day net difference (net loss) between the combined inflow and outflow copper discharges occurred at a streamflow of 14,800 ft³/s for Clark Fork above Missoula. For water samples collected on May 20, 2009, the copper discharge at Clark Fork above Missoula was 3.38 tons per day, and the combined copper discharges for Clark Fork at Turah Bridge and Blackfoot River near Bonner were 1.40 tons per day. The –1.98 tons per day net difference between the combined inflow and outflow copper discharges occurred at a streamflow of 15,400 ft³/s for Clark Fork above Missoula. Thus, for periodic water samples collected during similar streamflow magnitudes and conditions, the net loss of copper from the project area for the water year 2009 near-peak-flow sample set was about 17 percent of the net loss of copper from the project area for the water year 2008 near-peak-flow sample set.

In early water year 2009 (October 1–December 15, 2008), there was an approximate net balance between arsenic inflow and outflow loads, with an average daily net loss of less than 0.001 ton per day. During the period of ice conditions in mid-December 2008 through late January 2009, the cumulative net loss of arsenic from the project area was about 0.51 ton for an average of about 0.011 ton per day. After this erosional event, arsenic net losses decreased to about net balance conditions until the start of the runoff period in mid-March. During the water year 2009 runoff period (about March 9–July 27, 2009), net losses increased substantially; the cumulative net loss during the runoff period was about 3.1 tons of arsenic (average of about 0.022 ton per day). Average streamflow for Clark Fork above Missoula during the water year 2009 runoff period was 6,400 ft³/s. In comparison, during the water year 2008 runoff period (about March 9–August 10, 2008), the cumulative net loss was about 11.6 tons of arsenic (average of about 0.075 ton per day), and the average streamflow at Clark Fork above Missoula was about

5,430 ft³/s. After the water year 2009 runoff period, net losses persisted but decreased until the end of water year 2009. During the post-runoff period, the average daily net loss was about 0.010 ton per day.

Although there were substantial net losses of arsenic from the project area during the water year 2009 runoff period, the losses were much smaller than during the water year 2008 runoff period, even though streamflows were higher in water year 2009 than in water year 2008. This pattern is further illustrated by comparison of arsenic discharges associated with periodic water samples collected near the peak annual flows in water years 2008 and 2009. For water samples collected on May 19, 2008, at the three high-intensity stations that bracket the project area, the arsenic discharge at Clark Fork above Missoula was 1.04 tons per day, and the combined arsenic discharges for Clark Fork at Turah Bridge and Blackfoot River near Bonner were 0.210 ton per day. The –0.830 ton per day net difference (net loss) between the combined inflow and outflow arsenic discharges occurred at a streamflow of 14,800 ft³/s for Clark Fork above Missoula. For water samples collected on May 20, 2009, the arsenic discharge at Clark Fork above Missoula was 0.473 ton per day, and the combined arsenic discharges for Clark Fork at Turah Bridge and Blackfoot River near Bonner were 0.316 ton per day. The –0.157 ton per day net difference between the combined inflow and outflow arsenic discharges occurred at a streamflow of 15,400 ft³/s for Clark Fork above Missoula. Thus, for periodic water samples collected during similar streamflow magnitudes and conditions, the net loss of arsenic from the project area for the water year 2009 near-peak-flow sample set was about 19 percent of the net loss of arsenic from the project area for the water year 2008 near-peak-flow sample set.

Annual Loads and Mass Balance

Annual loads of suspended sediment and trace elements transported past each of the three high-intensity stations that bracket the Milltown Reservoir project area (table 5) were determined for water year 2009 by summing the estimated daily loads for the entire water year. Annual streamflow (in acre-ft) also is presented in table 5 to provide a perspective on streamflow conditions associated with constituent transport. Mass balance within the project area was determined as the difference between the combined annual inflow of streamflow and estimated loads from the two upstream source areas [basins upstream from Clark Fork at Turah Bridge (station 12334550) and Blackfoot River near Bonner (station 12340000)] and the annual outflow of streamflow and estimated loads at Clark Fork above Missoula (station 12340500).

In addition to results for water year 2009, annual loads and mass balances are presented for selected periods during water years 1985–2008 before and after the breach of Milltown Dam to provide a perspective on the effects of hydrologic conditions and the activities associated with the removal of Milltown Dam (table 5). The annual-loads and mass-balance data presented in table 5 include (1) average annual values for water years 1985–2005 (representing typical conditions during the period before the start of permanent drawdown of Milltown Reservoir on June 1, 2006); (2) average annual values for water years 1996–97 (representing high-flow conditions during the period before the start of permanent drawdown); (3) annual values for water years 2006 and 2007 (representing the period between the start of permanent drawdown of Milltown Reservoir and the breach of Milltown Dam; (4) annual values for water year 2008, during which Milltown Dam was breached; and (5) annual values for water year 2009 (the first full water year after the breach of Milltown Dam).

The annual (water year) period provides a convenient and consistent accounting period for comparing cumulative loads to discern changes in transport characteristics. The annual-loads and mass-balance data are segregated into discrete hydrologic periods or periods representing specific dam-removal activities, including the permanent drawdown of Milltown Reservoir and the breach of Milltown Dam, which affected constituent transport to and from the project area. However, the start of permanent drawdown (June 1, 2006) and the breach of Milltown Dam (March 28, 2008) did not coincide with the start of a given water year. For comparison purposes, water year 2006 was assigned to the period between the start of permanent drawdown and the breach of Milltown Dam because even though part of water year 2006 occurred before the start of permanent drawdown, the large effect of the drawdown conditions dominated the constituent transport conditions of the water year as a whole. Likewise, water year 2008 was assigned to the period after the breach of Milltown Dam because even though part of water year 2008 occurred before the breach of Milltown Dam, the large effect of the dam breach dominated the constituent transport conditions of the water year as a whole.

Comparison of annual mean streamflow between the various periods indicates substantial differences in streamflow conditions (table 2), which contributes to differences in constituent transport. During the period before the start of permanent drawdown, the mean annual streamflow of 2,550 ft³/s for water years 1985–2005 was less (88 percent) than the long-term mean annual streamflow of 2,910 ft³/s (table 2), but the mean annual streamflow of 4,540 ft³/s for the 1996–97 high-flow years was much greater (156 percent) than the long-term mean annual streamflow. For water years representing the period between the start of permanent drawdown and the breach of Milltown Dam (water years 2006–07), the mean annual streamflow of 2,460 ft³/s was less (85 percent) than the long-term mean annual streamflow and similar to the mean annual streamflow for water years 1985–2005. For water years representing the period after the breach of Milltown Dam (water years 2008–09), the annual mean streamflow of 3,040 ft³/s for water year 2008 was slightly greater (105 percent) than the long-term mean annual streamflow, and the annual mean streamflow of 3,560 ft³/s for water year 2009 was greater (122 percent) than the long-term mean annual streamflow. The annual mean streamflows for water years 2008 and

2009 were substantially smaller than the mean annual streamflow for water years 1996–97.

The mass balance of annual estimated loads for selected periods during water years 1985–2009 (table 5) provides an indication of variations in erosional and depositional processes within the project area. If less material was transported from the project area than entered, some of the suspended material entering the project area was deposited (net gain, indicated by positive values of mass balance). If more material was transported from the project area than entered, previously deposited sediment (and associated trace elements) within the project area was eroded and put into suspension, added to the suspended material entering the project area from upstream sources, and transported with the streamflow out of the project area (net loss, indicated by negative values of mass balance). The mass-balance results for the various periods indicate the differences in net gains or losses within the project area for distinctly different environmental settings and flow conditions.

The mass-balance results and percentages of the annual outflow transported from the project area that were contributed from the two upstream source areas and from within the project area during the various periods also are illustrated by using pie charts (fig. 12). The annual inflow loads contributed from individual upstream source areas are those shown for Clark Fork at Turah Bridge (station 12334550) and Blackfoot River near Bonner (station 12340000) in table 5. The annual loads contributed from within the project area are those shown as the mass balance in table 5, which represents the net loss from the project area. The annual outflow load transported from the project area is represented as the load transported past Clark Fork above Missoula (station 12340500). In some periods, there were net gains of streamflow volume or constituent loads within the project area. In these cases, the magnitudes of the net gains are shown in boxes beside the pie charts. Generally, the percent values shown in parentheses in figure 12 were calculated as the annual load contributed from an individual source area divided by the annual outflow load (values shown in fig. 12 and table 5) during the indicated period. However, in years when there were net gains of constituent loads within the project area, the net gains within the project area had to be accounted for in the calculations of the percent contribution from an individual source area to the annual outflow load. In years when there were net gains within the project area, the contribution from an individual source area to the net gain was assumed to be proportional to the contribution from the individual source area to the combined inflow to the project area. The percent values of source-area contributions were calculated as the annual load contributed from the individual source area minus the proportional contribution from the individual source area to the net gain divided by the annual outflow load. In addition to the proportional contributions indicated by percentages, the actual annual outflow loads [shown for Clark Fork above Missoula (station 12340500)] and source-area-contribution loads, in tons, are shown to provide perspective on the relative magnitude of differences in constituent loads transported during the various periods.

The size (area) of each pie chart (fig. 12) represents the total outflow from the project area at Clark Fork above Missoula, with colored areas indicating the relative contributions from each of three source areas. For each constituent column (that is, streamflow, suspended sediment, copper, and arsenic), the size of the pie chart representing a given annual value is sized proportionally to the largest annual value (or average annual value for multiple-year periods) within the constituent group. For example, in the suspended-sediment column, the largest annual outflow load was 510,000 tons in water year 2008; thus, the size of the water year 2008 pie chart for suspended sediment is the largest and serves as the reference for scaling the other suspended-sediment pie charts. The annual suspended-sediment-outflow load in water year 2009 was 221,000 tons, which is 43 percent of the water year 2008 annual outflow load. Thus, the size of the water year 2009 pie chart for suspended sediment is 43 percent of the size of the water year 2008 pie chart for suspended sediment. Differences

Table 5. Mass balance of annual streamflow and estimated loads of suspended sediment and unfiltered-recoverable trace elements transported to and from the Milltown Reservoir project area for selected periods during water years 1985–2009.

[Abbreviations: ND, not determined. All numerical values shown are rounded to three significant figures. In some cases, the combined inflow minus the outflow does not exactly equal the reported mass balance due to rounding effects. When calculating combined inflow or mass balance, all values used in the preliminary calculation were rounded to the same decimal place as three-significant-figure rounding of the smallest number used in the calculation. The final calculated value then was rounded to three significant figures]

Station name and number or summation category	Annual streamflow volume (acre-feet)	Estimated annual load (tons)							
		Suspended sediment	Cadmium[1]	Copper	Iron	Lead	Manganese	Zinc	Arsenic
Period before start of permanent drawdown of Milltown Reservoir and breach of Milltown Dam (water years 1985–2005)									
Average annual (water years 1985–2005)									
Clark Fork at Turah Bridge, near Bonner, Mont. (12334550)	856,000	52,700	ND	33.3	ND	7.02	ND	47.2	ND
Blackfoot River near Bonner, Mont. (12340000)	1,000,000	40,900	ND	4.87	ND	2.39	ND	6.74	ND
Combined inflow to Milltown Reservoir project area (sum of stations 12340000 and 12334550)	1,860,000	93,600	ND	38.2	ND	9.41	ND	53.9	ND
Milltown Reservoir project area outflow (as measured at the Clark Fork above Missoula, Mont. (12340500))	1,850,000	87,800	ND	34.1	ND	6.34	ND	56.3	ND
Mass balance for Milltown Reservoir project area: net gain (+) or loss (-)[2]	[3]**+14,300**	**+5,750**	**ND**	**+4.14**	**ND**	**+3.07**	**ND**	**-2.38**	**ND**
Average annual for selected high-streamflow years (water years 1996–97)									
Clark Fork at Turah Bridge, near Bonner, Mont. (12334550)	1,520,000	186,000	ND	97.0	ND	16.9	ND	146	ND
Blackfoot River near Bonner, Mont. (12340000)	1,740,000	142,000	ND	13.3	ND	3.05	ND	14.3	ND
Combined inflow to Milltown Reservoir project area (sum of stations 12340000 and 12334550)	3,260,000	328,000	ND	110	ND	19.9	ND	160	ND
Milltown Reservoir project area outflow (as measured at the Clark Fork above Missoula, Mont. (12340500))	3,280,000	381,000	ND	117	ND	22.3	ND	195	ND
Mass balance for Milltown Reservoir project area: net gain (+) or loss (-)[2]	**-25,000**	**-53,500**	**ND**	**-6.75**	**ND**	**-2.40**	**ND**	**-35.2**	**ND**

in the sizes of the pie charts are proportional to differences in annual values between years (or average annual values for multiple-year periods) in the total outflow streamflow volume or constituent loads. Also, differences in the sizes of the colored pie-chart slices for a given source area are proportional to differences between years (or multiple-year periods) in the contributions to the project area outflow from a given source area.

The largest streamflow was the average annual streamflow for water years 1996–97 (3,280 thousand acre-ft). The next largest annual streamflows were water year 2009 (2,580 thousand acre-ft) and water year 2008 (2,200 thousand acre-ft). Relative contributions of the two upstream source areas to the outflow streamflow generally were similar between all periods. The streamflow contribution of Clark Fork at Turah Bridge for the various periods ranged from 44

Table 5. Mass balance of annual streamflow and estimated loads of suspended sediment and unfiltered-recoverable trace elements transported to and from the Milltown Reservoir project area for selected periods during water years 1985–2009.—Continued

[Abbreviations: ND, not determined. All numerical values shown are rounded to three significant figures. In some cases, the combined inflow minus the outflow does not exactly equal the reported mass balance due to rounding effects. When calculating combined inflow or mass balance, all values used in the preliminary calculation were rounded to the same decimal place as three-significant-figure rounding of the smallest number used in the calculation. The final calculated value then was rounded to three significant figures]

Station name and number or summation category	Annual streamflow volume (acre-feet)	Estimated annual load (tons)							
		Suspended sediment	Cadmium[1]	Copper	Iron	Lead	Manganese	Zinc	Arsenic
Period between start of permanent drawdown of Milltown Reservoir and breach of Milltown Dam (water years 2006–07)									
Water year 2006[4]									
Clark Fork at Turah Bridge, near Bonner, Mont. (12334550)	794,000	33,300	0.132	18.6	555	3.23	73.5	26.7	8.60
Blackfoot River near Bonner, Mont. (12340000)	1,020,000	38,500	.0174	2.55	499	0.659	34.3	3.28	1.74
Combined inflow to Milltown Reservoir project area (sum of stations 12340000 and 12334550)	1,820,000	71,800	.149	21.2	1,050	3.89	108	30.0	10.3
Milltown Reservoir project area outflow (as measured at the Clark Fork above Missoula, Mont. (12340500))	1,800,000	97,700	.255	32.7	1,300	5.57	135	52.9	11.2
Mass balance for Milltown Reservoir project area: net gain (+) or loss (-)[2]	[3]+19,000	-25,900	-.106	-11.5	-250	-1.68	-27.0	-22.9	-0.900
Water year 2007									
Clark Fork at Turah Bridge, near Bonner, Mont. (12334550)	872,000	35,500	0.140	19.7	592	3.45	78.0	28.4	9.01
Blackfoot River near Bonner, Mont. (12340000)	946,000	23,000	.0160	2.03	312	0.420	24.2	2.66	1.64
Combined inflow to Milltown Reservoir project area (sum of stations 12340000 and 12334550)	1,820,000	58,500	.156	21.8	904	3.87	102	31.1	10.6
Milltown Reservoir project area outflow (as measured at the Clark Fork above Missoula, Mont. (12340500))	1,770,000	188,000	.453	58.8	1,880	9.67	189	105	16.7
Mass balance for Milltown Reservoir project area: net gain (+) or loss (-)[2]	[3]+49,000	-130,000	-.297	-37.0	-980	-5.80	-87.0	-74.0	-6.10

Table 5. Mass balance of annual streamflow and estimated loads of suspended sediment and unfiltered-recoverable trace elements transported to and from the Milltown Reservoir project area for selected periods during water years 1985–2009.—Continued

[Abbreviations: ND, not determined. All numerical values shown are rounded to three significant figures. In some cases, the combined inflow minus the outflow does not exactly equal the reported mass balance due to rounding effects. When calculating combined inflow or mass balance, all values used in the preliminary calculation were rounded to the same decimal place as three-significant-figure rounding of the smallest number used in the calculation. The final calculated value then was rounded to three significant figures]

Station name and number or summation category	Annual streamflow volume (acre-feet)	Estimated annual load (tons)							
		Suspended sediment	Cadmium[1]	Copper	Iron	Lead	Manga-nese	Zinc	Arsenic
Period after breach of Milltown Dam (water years 2008–09)									
Water year 2008[4]									
Clark Fork at Turah Bridge, near Bonner, Mont. (12334550)	1,070,000	56,800	0.185	27.2	923	5.37	113	40.3	12.2
Blackfoot River near Bonner, Mont. (12340000)	1,100,000	61,800	.0200	3.22	743	1.04	50.9	4.37	2.07
Combined inflow to Milltown Reservoir project area (sum of stations 12340000 and 12334550)	2,170,000	119,000	.205	30.4	1,670	6.41	164	44.7	14.3
Milltown Reservoir project area outflow (as measured at the Clark Fork above Missoula, Mont. (12340500))	2,200,000	510,000	1.14	188	4,640	28.9	338	290	27.5
Mass balance for Milltown Reservoir project area: net gain (+) or loss (-)[2]	**-30,000**	**-391,000**	**-.938**	**-157**	**-2,970**	**-22.5**	**-174**	**-245**	**-13.2**
Water year 2009									
Clark Fork at Turah Bridge, near Bonner, Mont. (12334550)	1,290,000	82,600	0.249	39.7	1,320	7.84	154	57.6	14.6
Blackfoot River near Bonner, Mont. (12340000)	1,270,000	61,800	.0182	3.47	762	1.06	53.2	4.96	2.26
Combined inflow to Milltown Reservoir project area (sum of stations 12340000 and 12334550)	2,560,000	144,000	.267	43.1	2,080	8.89	207	62.5	16.8
Milltown Reservoir project area outflow (as measured at the Clark Fork above Missoula, Mont. (12340500))	2,580,000	221,000	.478	72.1	2,530	12.3	259	111	21.1
Mass balance for Milltown Reservoir project area: net gain (+) or loss (-)[2]	**-20,000**	**-76,200**	**-0.211**	**-29.0**	**-446**	**-3.43**	**-52.4**	**-48.9**	**-4.27**

[1]Estimated cadmium loads for Blackfoot River near Bonner (station 12340000) were based on regression equations developed from datasets generally having more than 50 percent of the values censored (reported as less than the laboratory reporting level). Thus, estimated cadmium loads for this site have greater uncertainty than loads estimated for the other trace elements and the other two sites.

[2]Mass balance is the difference (net gain or loss) between the combined inflow to the Milltown Reservoir project area and the outflow transported from the Milltown Reservoir project area, as represented by Clark Fork above Missoula (station 12340500). Thus, a net gain (+) indicates net deposition in the Milltown Reservoir project area and a net loss (-) indicates net removal from the Milltown Reservoir project area.

[3]During some years, daily mean streamflow for Clark Fork above Missoula (station 12340500) was less than the combined inflow, which results in a calculated net gain of water in Milltown Reservoir. Rather than an actual gain of water (net storage), this calculated difference possibly represents a loss of surface water to the alluvium underlying Milltown Reservoir and the river reaches between the upstream and downstream gages, plus possible small amounts of evaporative loss from the reservoir surface.

[4]Although part of the given water year occurred outside of the indicated period, the given water year is assigned to the period most representative of the dominant conditions of that water year.

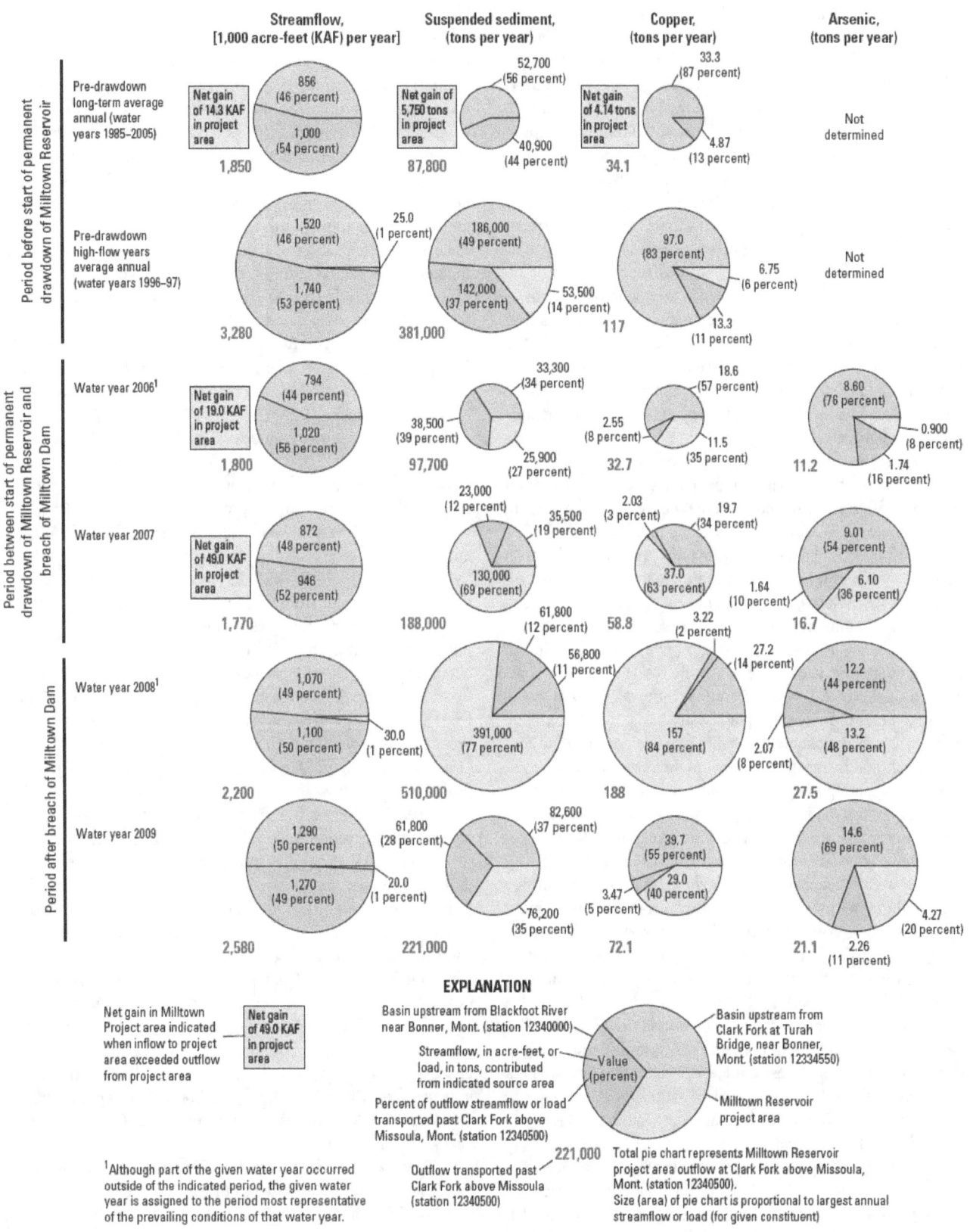

Figure 12. Annual streamflow volume and estimated loads of suspended sediment, unfiltered-recoverable copper, and unfiltered-recoverable arsenic contributed from upstream source areas and the Milltown Reservoir project area for selected time periods during water years 1985–2009.

to 50 percent of the outflow, and the streamflow contribution of Blackfoot River near Bonner ranged from 50 to 56 percent of the outflow. In all of the various periods, the net loss or gain of streamflow within the project area always was very minor, from 1 to 3 percent of the total outflow. Minor differences between combined inflow and outflow could represent inputs from ungaged small tributaries in the reaches between the streamflow-gaging stations, loss of surface water to groundwater in the alluvium underlying the project area, possible small amounts of evaporative loss from the reservoir surface, or minor inaccuracies in streamflow records.

Table 5 and figure 12 present a substantial amount of information concerning differences in suspended-sediment and trace-element transport characteristics, contributions from source areas, and mass balance within the project area for the various years (or multiple-year periods). Selected observations on some of the most prominent features regarding load magnitudes, source-area contributions, and mass balance are presented below.

During the pre-drawdown period (water years 1985–2005), there was an average annual net gain of suspended sediment (5,750 tons) in the project area, but relatively substantial annual net loss (53,500 tons) during the high-flow years of 1996–97 (table 5). This pattern illustrates the long-term effect of Milltown Dam on suspended-sediment transport. Milltown Reservoir was relatively shallow, providing limited storage capacity for sediment deposition and susceptible to bed and bank erosion by high-velocity streamflows or ice conditions. During the period 1908–2005 when the reservoir was operated as "run-of-the-river," with streamflow inflows generally about equal to streamflow outflows on a daily basis, an approximate equilibrium or net balance probably had been established for constituent loads transported through the reservoir under long-term average streamflow conditions (for example, average sediment inflow loads probably were about equal to average sediment outflow loads). Mean annual streamflow for Clark Fork above Missoula during water years 1985–2005 (table 2) was below (88 percent) the long-term mean annual streamflow. During these below-normal streamflow years, below-normal hydraulic energies within the Milltown Reservoir resulted in net gain (deposition) of sediment transported into the reservoir. However, during the above-normal streamflow conditions during water years 1996–97 (which were the 3rd and 6th largest annual mean streamflows during the 1930–2009 period of record for Clark Fork above Missoula), the above-normal hydraulic energies resulted in a relatively large net loss of sediment from the reservoir. Also, net losses in water year 1996 were affected by scouring caused by substantial ice-formation and rapid breakup.

When the "run-of-the-river" equilibrium was altered by the start of permanent drawdown in June 2006, net losses of sediment from the project area increased immediately (fig. 9). During the period between the start of permanent drawdown and the breach of Milltown Dam, the environment of Milltown Reservoir was markedly altered by the steeper hydraulic gradient that resulted from reducing the typical reservoir

water level by about 10 to 12 ft. The effect of this alteration was substantially greater contributions of load from within the project area relative to pre-drawdown conditions. The contributions from within the project area are represented by the net loss determined in the mass-balance calculations. For example, in water year 2007 (the first full water year after the start of permanent drawdown), the annual contribution of suspended sediment from within the project area (130,000 tons; table 5, fig. 12) during below average (84 percent) streamflow conditions was about 2.4 times larger than the average annual contribution (53,500 tons) from within the project area during the high-flow years 1996–97. Further, water year 2007 was the first water year that the contribution of suspended sediment from within the project area to the total outflow (69 percent of outflow load) was larger than the combined contributions from the two upstream source areas represented by the basins upstream from Clark Fork at Turah Bridge and Blackfoot River near Bonner.

The activities associated with the breach of Milltown Dam on March 28, 2008, further altered the project area environment and resulted in a large increase in net losses of suspended sediment from the project area. The Clark Fork water-surface elevation was lowered by an additional 15 ft, and the project area essentially was changed from reservoir to free-flowing river conditions. The annual contribution of suspended sediment from within the project area during water year 2008 (391,000 tons) was by far the largest of any year during the monitoring period (77 percent of outflow load) and occurred during slightly above-average streamflow conditions. However, the annual contribution of suspended sediment from the project area during water year 2009 (76,200 tons) was substantially smaller than those in water years 2007 (130,000 tons) and 2008 (391,000 tons) even though streamflow was larger in water year 2009 than in water years 2007 and 2008. Thus, there was substantial depletion of the project area sediment supply by the end of water year 2008.

Interannual variability in copper transport was very similar to interannual variability in suspended-sediment transport. In water year 2007, the contribution of copper from the project area (37.0 tons) was about 5.5 times larger than the average annual contribution during 1996–97 (6.75 tons). The annual contribution of copper from the project area during water year 2008 (157 tons) was the largest of any year during the monitoring period (84 percent of the outflow load). The annual contribution of copper from the project area during water year 2009 (29.0 tons) was substantially smaller than those in water years 2007 (37.0 tons) and 2008 (157 tons), even though streamflow was larger in water year 2009 than in water years 2007 and 2008.

There were distinct differences in temporal variability of both total outflow loads from the project area and relative contributions from source areas for arsenic compared to suspended sediment and copper (fig. 12). The basin upstream from Clark Fork at Turah Bridge accounted for the largest percent contribution of arsenic to the project area outflow from any upstream source area for all water years except

2008 (table 5). For all water years, contributions of arsenic from within the project area were smaller than the combined contributions from the two upstream source areas represented by the basins upstream from Clark Fork at Turah Bridge and Blackfoot River near Bonner. Differences in the patterns of load contributions for arsenic relative to the other trace elements probably are attributable to the greater percentage of arsenic that occurs in the dissolved phase relative to the other trace elements in the Clark Fork. Thus, the relatively small percentage of arsenic in the particulate phase could have resulted in less historical deposition within the project area and a smaller percentage of arsenic contributed from within the project area relative to the other trace elements. Also, arsenic potentially could have been mobilized from the sediment that was deposited in Milltown Reservoir to groundwater of the underlying alluvial aquifer (U.S. Environmental Protection Agency, 2004), thereby depleting the sediment of some of the original arsenic content. Annual contributions of arsenic from within the project area during water years 2007 and 2008 were 6.10 and 13.2 tons, respectively. The annual contribution of arsenic from within the project area during water year 2009 (4.27 tons) was smaller than water years 2007 and 2008. The relative reduction in the contribution of arsenic from within the project area between water year 2008 and water year 2009 was substantial, but not as large as other trace elements. The different chemical and transport characteristics of arsenic relative to the other trace elements might have caused different spatial deposition patterns in the former Milltown Reservoir or different responses to the altered hydrologic conditions caused by dam-removal activities, and resulted in different transport characteristics for arsenic than for the other trace elements during water years 2008 and 2009.

The cumulative loads of constituents contributed from within the project area (shown as mass-balance net losses in table 5) during the remediation activities associated with the removal of Milltown Dam (that is, from the start of permanent drawdown on June 1, 2006, to the end of water year 2009) are presented in figure 13. The estimated cumulative loads of suspended sediment, copper, and arsenic contributed from within the project area during June 1, 2006–September 30, 2009 were 623,000, 235, and 26.8 tons, respectively. Temporal variability in constituent transport from the project area and the effect of runoff or remediation activities on constituent transport are apparent in figure 13. During the permanent drawdown period (June 1, 2006–March 27, 2008), the cumulative loads of suspended sediment, copper, and arsenic contributed from within the project area were 172,000 tons, 56.1 tons, and 10.6 tons, respectively. From March 28, 2008 (when Milltown Dam was breached), until the end of water year 2008, the additional loads of suspended sediment, copper, and arsenic contributed from within the project area were 375,000 tons, 150 tons, and 11.9 tons, respectively. The largest and most abrupt increase in loads contributed from within the project area occurred in the first 3 months after the breach of Milltown Dam (fig. 13). During water year 2009, the additional loads of suspended sediment, copper, and arsenic contributed from within the project

area were 76,200 tons, 29.0 tons, and 4.27 tons, respectively. The much smaller contributions of constituent loads during water year 2009 relative to the drawdown period and the post-breach period of water year 2008 provide further evidence of the substantial depletion of constituent supply within the project area during the drawdown period and water year 2008.

During the years of the most substantial remediation activities (that is, water year 2007, when permanent drawdown was conducted for the entire year, and water year 2008, when Milltown Dam was breached) constituent loads relative to streamflow were proportionately larger than other years, and the relative contributions of constituents from within the project area also were larger than other years (fig. 12). The relative contributions of constituents from source areas during water years 2006 and 2009 (before and after the most substantial remediation activities) generally were similar. Thus, in a relatively short time frame after the start of the most substantial remediation activities (that is, the period from the start of permanent drawdown on June 1, 2006, to the end of water year 2008, during which two complete annual runoff periods occurred), constituent transport characteristics in the Clark Fork near the project area appear to be approaching typical conditions observed before the breach of Milltown Dam. However, remediation and restoration activities that occur after the end of water year 2009 might affect the apparent temporal pattern in constituent transport characteristics, for example, the diversion of the Clark Fork from the constructed bypass channel to a new channel that occurred in December 2010 (*http://www.epa.gov/region8/ superfund/mt/milltown/UpdateDecember2010.pdf*, accessed February 22, 2011). Adjustment of the Clark Fork to a new geomorphic environment might alter patterns in constituent transport characteristics.

Estimated Loads Transported Through the Clark Fork Downstream from the Milltown Reservoir Project Area

Primary objectives for the investigation of transport characteristics through the Clark Fork downstream from the Milltown Reservoir project area include (1) estimating annual loads and source-area contributions to the Clark Fork downstream from the confluence with the Flathead River (hereinafter referred to as the lower Clark Fork outflow), and (2) determining the mass balance of suspended-sediment and trace-element loads for an extensive main-stem reach (about 87 mi long) of the Clark Fork between the project area outflow at Clark Fork above Missoula (station 12340500, fig. 1, map number 4) and the Clark Fork at St. Regis (station 12354500, fig. 1, map number 6). Annual loads of suspended sediment and trace elements transported past each of the three low-intensity stations downstream from the project area outflow (fig. 1, sites 5–7, table 6) were estimated for water years

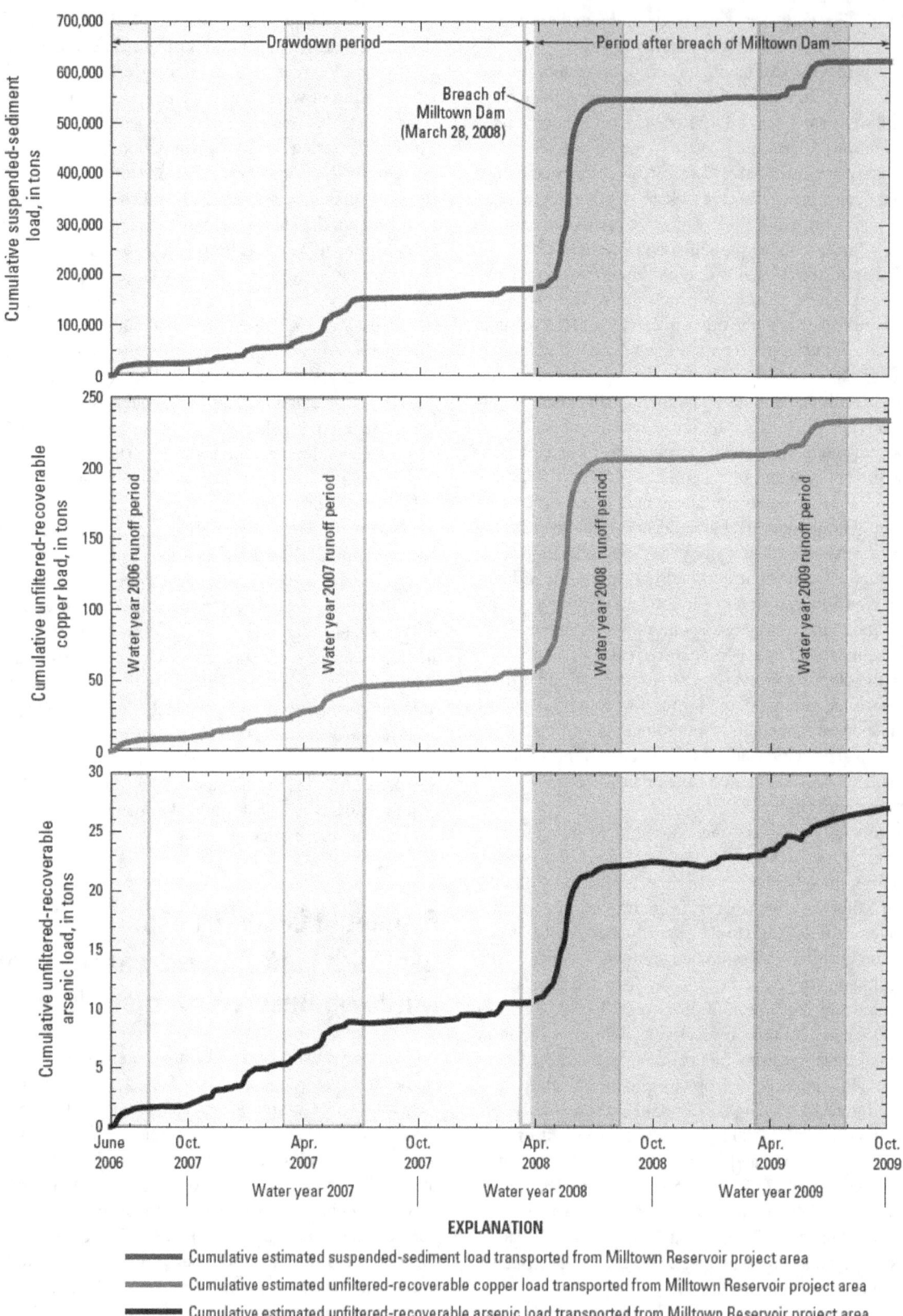

Figure 13.   Cumulative estimated loads of suspended sediment, unfiltered-recoverable copper, and unfiltered-recoverable arsenic contributed from the Milltown Reservoir project area during the period June 1, 2006 (start of permanent drawdown), through water year 2009.

2006–09 by summing the estimated daily loads for each entire water year. Annual streamflow (in acre-ft) also is presented in table 6 to provide a perspective on streamflow conditions associated with constituent transport. Most of the load estimates presented in table 6 for the low-intensity stations have greater uncertainties than load estimates for the high-intensity stations bracketing the project area. For the data in table 6, emphasis generally is placed on relative comparison of results between stations and years, rather than on the absolute magnitude of load estimates.

Mass balance of constituent loads within the 87-mi main-stem reach of the Clark Fork between Clark Fork above Missoula and Clark Fork at St. Regis was determined as the difference between the combined inflow of the two gaged upstream source areas (that is, the project area outflow at Clark Fork above Missoula and the Bitterroot River near Missoula) and the reach outflow (Clark Fork at St. Regis) for water years 2006–09. The two gaged source areas account for about 82 percent of the drainage area and about 74 percent of the mean annual streamflow at the Clark Fork at St. Regis. Mass-balance calculations for this extensive main-stem reach provide general information on transport of constituents (much of which were contributed from the Milltown Reservoir project area) in the lower Clark Fork downstream from the project area outflow. It is notable that there are somewhat substantial tributary inputs (about 18 percent of the drainage area and about 26 percent of the mean annual streamflow) to the reach that were not gaged or monitored for water quality. Thus, the mass-balance calculations for the main-stem reach reflect (1) a complete accounting of the main-stem inflows to the reach that represent about 56 percent of the drainage area and 41 percent of the mean annual inflows to the reach, (2) a complete accounting of the largest single tributary inflow to the reach (Bitterroot River) that represents about 26 percent of the drainage area and 33 percent of the mean annual inflows, and (3) an incomplete accounting of the interaction between net gains or losses of constituents within the Clark Fork channel and the undetermined contribution from ungaged tributary source areas (including the city of Missoula) that represent about 18 percent of the drainage area and about 26 percent of the mean annual inflows. Because of the uncertainty in distinguishing the total load input to the reach, net gains or losses for the reach are only generally characterized and detailed determination of the fate of materials from the project area outflow to the reach is not possible. However, the mass-balance calculations for the main-stem reach provide general information on temporal variability in constituent transport in the reach and relative contributions from the two gaged source areas.

The annual (water year) period provides a convenient and consistent accounting period for comparing cumulative loads to discern temporal changes in transport characteristics. However, water-quality sampling for the low-intensity stations was restricted to the runoff periods of each water year. Thus, it was necessary to extend the regression relations developed using the runoff period data to substantial periods outside the runoff periods when no data were collected. The potential errors associated with extending the regression relations probably are small because (1) data collected on the fringes of the runoff periods (which generally were near base-flow conditions) probably provide a reasonably accurate representation of nonrunoff conditions in the regression relations, and (2) periods outside of the annual runoff period typically accounted for a relatively small part of the annual loads. During water years 2006–09, an average of about 10 percent of the annual suspended-sediment loads at Clark Fork above Missoula (a daily suspended-sediment station) was transported during periods outside of the annual runoff period, illustrating the relatively small percentage of constituent loads that is transported during nonrunoff conditions.

For water years representing the permanent drawdown period (water years 2006–07), the mean annual streamflow of 6,300 ft^3/s at Clark Fork at St. Regis (table 3) was less (86 percent) than the long-term mean annual streamflow. For water years representing the period after the breach of Milltown Dam (water years 2008–09), the mean annual streamflow of 7,710 ft^3/s was slightly greater (106 percent) than the long-term mean annual streamflow.

The annual outflow loads transported past the Clark Fork downstream from the confluence with the Flathead River and relative contributions from the individual source areas are illustrated by using pie charts (fig. 14). The estimated percentages of the loads for Clark Fork above Missoula contributed from within the Milltown Reservoir project area also are indicated to provide information on the effect of the Milltown Dam removal activities on constituent transport characteristics downstream from the project area outflow. The annual inflow loads contributed from the gaged upstream source areas (table 6) are those shown for Clark Fork above Missoula (station 12340500), Bitterroot River near Missoula (station 12352500), and Flathead River at Perma (station 12388700). The annual loads contributed from the main-stem reach are those shown as negative values (net loss) for the mass balance in table 6; positive values of mass balance represent net gains or deposition within the main-stem reach. In years when there were net gains of constituent loads within the main-stem reach, the magnitudes of the net gains are shown in boxes beside the pies (fig. 14), or as positive mass-balance values (table 6). The percent values of source-area contributions were calculated as the annual load contributed from an individual source area divided by the annual lower Clark Fork outflow load (calculated as the sum of Clark Fork at St. Regis and Flathead River at Perma in table 6) during the indicated period. In years when there were net gains of constituent loads within the main-stem reach, the contribution from an individual source area to the net gain was assumed to be proportional to the contribution from the individual source area to the combined inflow to the main-stem reach. In years when there were net gains, the percent values of source-area contributions were calculated as the annual load contributed from the individual source area minus the proportional contribution from the individual source area to the net gain divided

Table 6.   Mass balance of annual streamflow and estimated loads of suspended sediment and unfiltered-recoverable trace elements transported to the Clark Fork downstream from the confluence with the Flathead River during water years 2006–09.

[Abbreviations: ND, not determined. All numerical values shown are rounded to three significant figures. In some cases, the combined inflow minus the outflow does not exactly equal the reported mass balance due to rounding effects. When calculating combined inflow or mass balance, all values used in the preliminary calculation were rounded to the same decimal place as three-significant-figure rounding of the smallest number used in the calculation. The final calculated value then was rounded to three significant figures]

Station name and number or summation category	Annual streamflow volume (acre-feet)	Estimated annual load (tons)							
		Suspended sediment	Cadmium[1]	Copper[1]	Iron	Lead	Manga-nese	Zinc[1]	Arsenic
Period between start of permanent drawdown of Milltown Reservoir and breach of Milltown Dam (water years 2006–07)									
Water year 2006[2]									
Milltown Reservoir project area outflow (as measured at the Clark Fork above Missoula, Mont. (12340500))	1,800,000	97,700	0.255	32.7	1,300	5.57	135	52.9	11.2
Bitterroot River near Missoula, Mont. (12352500)	1,570,000	100,000	.0210	3.33	1,180	1.12	54.6	5.65	1.02
Combined inflow to main-stem reach of Clark Fork (sum of Clark Fork above Missoula (12340500) and Bitterroot River near Missoula, Mont. (12352500))	3,370,000	198,000	.276	36.0	2,480	6.69	190	58.6	12.2
Clark Fork at St. Regis, Mont. (12354500)	4,750,000	331,000	.389	48.3	3,420	9.5	256	80.7	16.7
Mass balance for main-stem reach of Clark Fork (difference between combined inflow to the main-stem reach of the Clark Fork and the Clark Fork at St. Regis): net gain (+) or loss (-)[3]	**-1,380,000**	**-133,000**	**-.113**	**-12.3**	**-940**	**-2.81**	**-66.4**	**-22.2**	**-4.48**
Flathead River near Perma, Mont. (12388700)	9,190,000	64,500	ND[4]	6.02	920	1.21	68.4	6.42	5.97
Lower Clark Fork outflow (sum of Clark Fork at St. Regis (12354500) and the Flathead River near Perma (12388700)	13,900,000	395,000	ND[4]	54.3	4,340	10.7	324	87.1	22.7
Water year 2007									
Milltown Reservoir project area outflow (as measured at the Clark Fork above Missoula, Mont. (12340500))	1,770,000	188,000	0.453	58.8	1,880	9.67	189	105	16.7
Bitterroot River near Missoula, Mont. (12352500)	1,400,000	44,500	.0153	1.94	664	.556	32.9	3.82	0.864
Combined inflow to main-stem reach of Clark Fork (sum of Clark Fork above Missoula (12340500) and Bitterroot River near Missoula, Mont. (12352500))	3,170,000	233,000	.468	60.7	2,540	10.2	222	109	17.6
Clark Fork at St. Regis, Mont. (12354500)	4,370,000	163,000	.322	42.0	2,170	7.23	204	69.7	15.6

Table 6.   Mass balance of annual streamflow and estimated loads of suspended sediment and unfiltered-recoverable trace elements transported to the Clark Fork downstream from the confluence with the Flathead River during water years 2006–09.—Continued

[Abbreviations: ND, not determined. All numerical values shown are rounded to three significant figures. In some cases, the combined inflow minus the outflow does not exactly equal the reported mass balance due to rounding effects. When calculating combined inflow or mass balance, all values used in the preliminary calculation were rounded to the same decimal place as three-significant-figure rounding of the smallest number used in the calculation. The final calculated value then was rounded to three significant figures]

Station name and number or summation category	Annual streamflow volume (acre-feet)	Estimated annual load (tons)							
		Suspended sediment	Cadmium[1]	Copper[1]	Iron	Lead	Manga-nese	Zinc[1]	Arsenic
Period between start of permanent drawdown of Milltown Reservoir and breach of Milltown Dam (water years 2006-07)—Continued									
Water year 2007—Continued									
Mass balance for main-stem reach of Clark Fork (difference between combined inflow to the main-stem reach of the Clark Fork and the Clark Fork at St. Regis): net gain (+) or loss (-)[3]	**-1,200,000**	**+70,000**	**+.146**	**+18.7**	**+374**	**+3.00**	**+17.9**	**+39.1**	**+1.96**
Flathead River near Perma, Mont. (12388700)	7,920,000	38,800	ND[4]	4.61	632	.888	52.0	4.89	5.16
Lower Clark Fork outflow (sum of Clark Fork at St. Regis (12354500) and the Flathead River near Perma (12388700)	12,300,000	202,000	ND[4]	46.6	2,800	8.12	257	74.6	20.8
Period after breach of Milltown Dam (water years 2008–09)									
Water year 2008[2]									
Milltown Reservoir project area outflow (as measured at the Clark Fork above Missoula, Mont. (12340500))	2,200,000	510,000	1.14	188	4,640	28.9	338	290	27.5
Bitterroot River near Missoula, Mont. (12352500)	1,910,000	123,000	.0246	4.14	1,320	1.31	62.4	6.39	1.20
Combined inflow to main-stem reach of Clark Fork (sum of Clark Fork above Missoula (12340500) and Bitterroot River near Missoula, Mont. (12352500))	4,110,000	633,000	1.16	192	5,960	30.2	400	296	28.7
Clark Fork at St. Regis, Mont. (12354500)	5,510,000	562,000	1.34	208	6,870	33.0	471	332	31.3
Mass balance for main-stem reach of Clark Fork (difference between combined inflow to the main-stem reach of the Clark Fork and the Clark Fork at St. Regis): net gain (+) or loss (-)[3]	**-1,400,000**	**+70,500**	**-.175**	**-15.9**	**-910**	**-2.79**	**-71.0**	**-35.6**	**-2.60**
Flathead River near Perma, Mont. (12388700)	8,720,000	87,700	ND[4]	8.04	1,240	1.54	79.0	8.49	6.19
Lower Clark Fork outflow (sum of Clark Fork at St. Regis (12354500) and the Flathead River near Perma (12388700)	14,300,000	650,000	ND[4]	217	8,110	34.6	550	341	37.5

Table 6. Mass balance of annual streamflow and estimated loads of suspended sediment and unfiltered-recoverable trace elements transported to the Clark Fork downstream from the confluence with the Flathead River during water years 2006–09.—Continued

[Abbreviations: ND, not determined. All numerical values shown are rounded to three significant figures. In some cases, the combined inflow minus the outflow does not exactly equal the reported mass balance due to rounding effects. When calculating combined inflow or mass balance, all values used in the preliminary calculation were rounded to the same decimal place as three-significant-figure rounding of the smallest number used in the calculation. The final calculated value then was rounded to three significant figures]

Station name and number or summation category	Annual streamflow volume (acre-feet)	Estimated annual load (tons)							
		Suspended sediment	Cadmium[1]	Copper[1]	Iron	Lead	Manga-nese	Zinc[1]	Arsenic
Period after breach of Milltown Dam (water years 2008–09)—Continued									
Water year 2009									
Milltown Reservoir project area outflow (as measured at the Clark Fork above Missoula, Mont. (12340500))	2,580,000	221,000	0.478	72.1	2,530	12.3	259	111	21.1
Bitterroot River near Missoula, Mont. (12352500)	1,950,000	134,000	.0265	4.30	1,490	1.49	70.4	7.10	1.21
Combined inflow to main-stem reach of Clark Fork (sum of Clark Fork above Missoula (12340500) and Bitterroot River near Missoula, Mont. (12352500))	4,530,000	354,000	.505	76.4	4,020	13.8	330	118	22.3
Clark Fork at St. Regis, Mont. (12354500)	5,660,000	551,000	.536	88.2	5,360	17.5	367	134	22.4
Mass balance for main-stem reach of Clark Fork (difference between combined inflow to the main-stem reach of the Clark Fork and the Clark Fork at St. Regis): net gain (+) or loss (-)[3]	**-1,130,000**	**-196,000**	**-.032**	**-11.8**	**-1,340**	**-3.71**	**-38.0**	**-15.8**	**-0.090**
Flathead River near Perma, Mont. (12388700)	6,970,000	30,300	ND[4]	3.88	516	.714	44.2	4.11	4.68
Lower Clark Fork outflow (sum of Clark Fork at St. Regis (12354500) and the Flathead River near Perma (12388700))	12,700,000	581,000	ND[4]	92.1	5,870	18.2	411	138	27.1

[1]Estimated loads for some trace-element and station combinations (including cadmium for stations 12340000, 12352500, and 12388700, and copper and zinc for station 12388700) were based on regression equations developed from datasets generally having more than 50 percent of the values censored (reported as less than the laboratory reporting level). Thus, estimated loads for these trace-element and station combinations have greater uncertainty than loads estimated for the other trace-element and station combinations.

[2]Although part of the given water year occurred outside of the indicated period, the given water year is assigned to the period most representative of the prevailing conditions of that water year.

[3]Mass balance is the difference (net gain or loss) between the combined inflow to the main-stem reach of the Clark Fork between the confluence with the Bitterroot River and Clark Fork at St. Regis and the outflow transported from the reach at Clark Fork at St. Regis (station 12354500). Thus, a net gain (+) indicates net deposition in the reach and a net loss (-) indicates net removal from the reach.

[4]Cadmium loads for station 12388700 (and calculated values dependent on those loads) were not determined because the large percent of censored values (94.4 percent; table 4) precluded the use of any method for estimating censored concentrations.

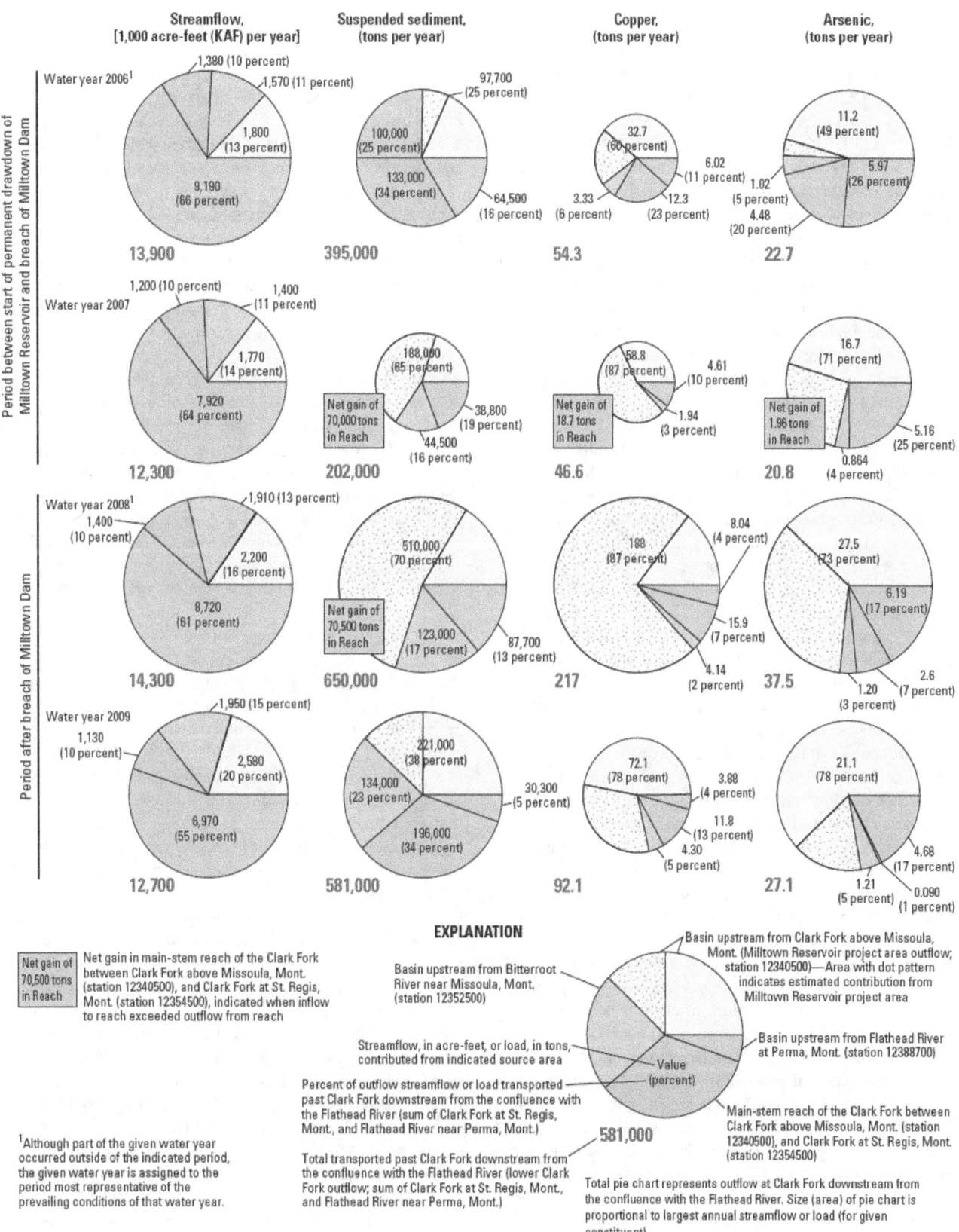

Figure 14. Annual streamflow and estimated loads of suspended sediment, unfiltered-recoverable copper, and unfiltered-recoverable arsenic for the Clark Fork downstream from the confluence with the Flathead River and contributions from upstream source areas, water years 2006–09.

by the annual lower Clark Fork outflow load. In addition to the percent values, the estimated total lower Clark Fork outflow loads, contributions from the gaged source area, and contributions from the intervening main-stem reach, in tons, are shown to provide perspective on the large differences in constituent loads transported during the various periods.

The effects of the Milltown Dam removal activities are apparent in the temporal variability of relative contributions of estimated annual suspended-sediment loads from source areas to the lower Clark Fork downstream from the project area outflow. During the years of the most substantial remediation activities (that is, water year 2007, when permanent drawdown was conducted for the entire year, and water year 2008 when Milltown Dam was breached), the estimated annual loads for the Clark Fork above Missoula (project area outflow) accounted for a large percentage (65 percent for water year 2007 and 70 percent for water year 2008) of the suspended-sediment load transported past the lower Clark Fork outflow. During water years 2006 and 2009 (before and after the most substantial remediation activities), the Clark Fork above Missoula accounted for substantially smaller percentages (25 percent for water year 2006 and 38 percent for water year 2009) of the suspended-sediment load transported past the lower Clark Fork outflow than in water years 2007–08. Also, the relative contributions of suspended sediment from source areas during water years 2006 and 2009 generally were similar. Thus in a relatively short time frame after the start of the most substantial remediation activities (that is, the period from the start of permanent drawdown on June 1, 2006, to the end of water year 2008, during which two full annual runoff periods occurred), relative contributions of suspended sediment from upstream source areas to the lower Clark Fork appear to be approaching typical conditions observed before the breach of Milltown Dam. However, remediation and restoration activities that occur after the end of water year 2009, might affect the apparent temporal pattern in source-area contributions of suspended sediment to the lower Clark Fork, for example, the diversion of the Clark Fork from the constructed bypass channel to a new channel that occurred in December 2010 (*http://www.epa.gov/region8/superfund/mt/milltown/UpdateDecember2010.pdf*, accessed February 22, 2011). Adjustment of the Clark Fork to a new geomorphic environment might alter patterns in source-area contributions of suspended sediment to the lower Clark Fork.

The effects of the Milltown Dam removal activities also are apparent in the temporal variability in net gains and losses of suspended sediment in the main-stem reach during water years 2006–09. During the years of the most substantial remediation activities (water years 2007 and 2008), there were net gains of suspended sediment in the intervening main-stream reach. During water years 2006 and 2009, there were net losses of suspended sediment from the main-stem reach (fig. 14, table 6).

Temporal variability in the particle-size composition (that is, the percent of fines and sand) of suspended sediment in the inflow to and outflow from the main-stem reach provides general information on the potential processes affecting variability in gain or loss of suspended sediment in the reach. The average annual particle-size composition for the combined inflow to and outflow from the main-stem reach was estimated using the particle-size composition and instantaneous suspended-sediment loads of concurrent periodic water-quality samples. The loads of fines for all concurrent samples collected during a given year for the combined inflow were summed to determine the cumulative load of fines for the concurrent water-quality samples for the combined inflow for the given year. The loads of suspended sediment for all concurrent samples collected during a given year for the combined inflow were summed to determine the cumulative load of suspended sediment for the concurrent water-quality samples for the combined inflow for the given year. The cumulative load of fines for the concurrent water-quality samples for the given year was divided by the cumulative load of suspended sediment to estimate the annual load-weighted percent fines for the combined inflow for the given year. The annual load-weighted percent sand was estimated by subtracting the annual load-weighted percent fines from 100 percent. The same procedures were used to estimate the annual load-weighted percent fines and percent sand for the outflow from the main-stem reach. The annual load-weighted percent fines and sand for the combined inflow to and outflow from the main-stem reach for water years 2006–09 are presented in figure 15. The estimated annual load-weighted percent fines and sand were multiplied by the annual estimated suspended-sediment loads (table 6) to estimate annual loads of fines and sands (table 7). These loads, by particle size, illustrate variability in net transport of fines and sand through the main-stem reach during water years 2006–09.

During water year 2006, streamflow at Clark Fork at St. Regis was below normal (table 3) and suspended sediment in the combined gaged inflow to the main-stem reach was estimated to be 53.3-percent fines, and the suspended sediment in the outflow from the main-stem reach was estimated to be 54.9-percent fines (fig. 15). Thus, suspended sediment in the inflow to and outflow from the main-stem reach consisted of generally similar percentages of sand and fines. There was an estimated net loss of both fines and sand from the main-stem reach in water year 2006 (table 7). During water year 2007, streamflow at Clark Fork at St. Regis was below normal (table 3) and suspended sediment in the combined gaged inflow to the main-stem reach was 35.5-percent fines, and the suspended sediment in the outflow from the main-stem reach was 61.6-percent fines (fig. 15). Thus, suspended sediment in the combined inflow to the main-stem reach was predominantly sand (64.5 percent), and the suspended sediment in the outflow from the main-stem reach was predominantly fines (61.6 percent) in water year 2007. There was an estimated net loss of fines (about 17,300 tons) from the main-stem reach, but a larger net gain (deposition) of sand (about 87,400 tons) in the main-stem reach in water year 2007 (table 7). The hydraulic energies in the Clark Fork during the below normal streamflow conditions of water year 2007 probably were sufficient

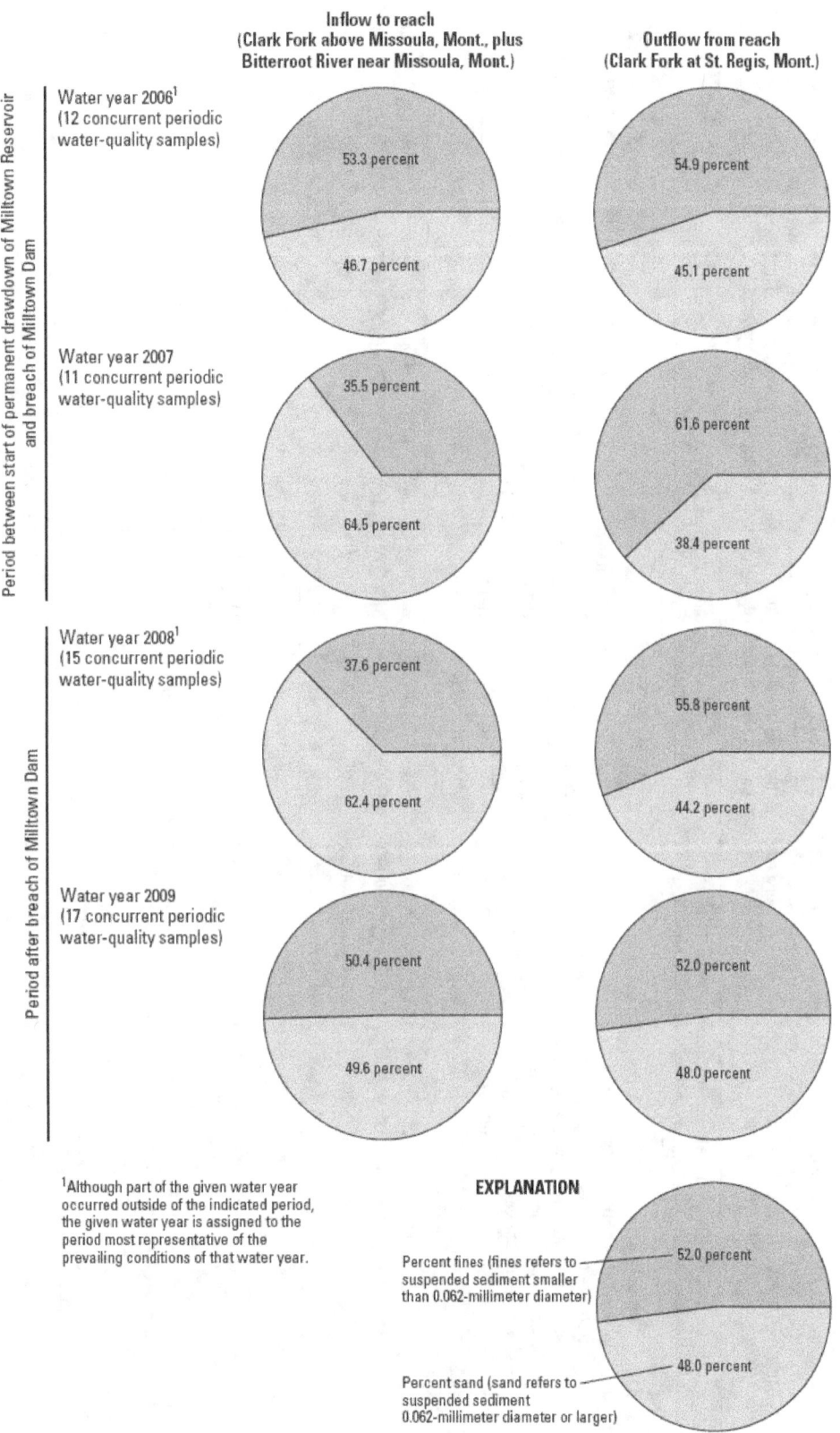

Figure 15. Percent of fines and sand in the cumulative loads of suspended sediment for concurrent periodic water-quality samples for the combined inflow to and outflow from the main-stem reach of the Clark Fork from the Clark Fork above Missoula to the Clark Fork at St. Regis, water years 2006–09.

Table 7.   Estimated annual loads and mass balance of various size classes of suspended sediment transported to and from the main-stem reach of the Clark Fork above Missoula to the Clark Fork at St. Regis during water years 2006–09.

[Main-stream reach refers to the Clark Fork from the Clark Fork above Missoula to the Clark Fork at St. Regis. Fines refers to suspended sediment smaller than 0.062-millimeter diameter. Sand refers to suspended sediment 0.062-millimeter diameter or larger. All numerical values shown are rounded to three significant figures. In some cases, the summation of the mass balance for fines and the mass balance for sand does not exactly equal the total mass balance due to rounding effects. When calculating total mass balance, all values used in the preliminary calculation were rounded to the same decimal place as three-significant-figure rounding of the smallest number used in the calculation. The final calculated value then was rounded to three significant figures. Abbreviations: USGS, U.S. Geological Survey]

Water year	Number of concurrent periodic water-quality samples	Combined inflow to main-stem reach (Clark Fork above Missoula, Mont., plus Bitterroot River near Missoula, Mont.)					Outflow from main-stem reach (Clark Fork at St. Regis, Mont.)					Mass balance for main-stem reach of the Clark Fork above Missoula and the Clark Fork at St. Regis: net gain (+; no shading) or loss (-; grey shading)[3]		
		Particle-size composition of the cumulative suspended-sediment load for concurrent periodic water-quality samples[1]		Estimated annual suspended-sediment load (table 6)	Estimated annual fines load[2]	Estimated annual sand load[2]	Particle-size composition of cumulative suspended-sediment load for concurrent periodic water-quality samples[1]		Estimated annual suspended-sediment load (table 6)	Estimated annual fines load[2]	Estimated annual sand load[2]	Fines	Sand	Total
		Percent fines	Percent sand				Percent fines	Percent sand						
2006	12	53.3	46.7	198,000	105,000	92,600	54.9	45.1	331,000	182,000	149,000	-77,000	-56,400	-133,000
2007	11	35.5	64.5	233,000	82,700	150,000	61.6	38.4	163,000	100,000	62,600	-17,300	+87,400	+70,000
2008	15	37.6	62.4	633,000	238,000	395,000	55.8	44.2	562,000	313,000	249,000	-75,000	+146,000	+70,500
2009	17	50.4	49.6	354,000	178,000	176,000	52.0	48.0	551,000	286,000	264,000	-108,000	-88,000	-196,000

[1]For each station, the particle-size composition of the cumulative suspended-sediment load for concurrent water-quality samples collected during a given year was calculated by:

(1) multiplying the percentage of fines by the suspended-sediment load to determine the fines load for each concurrent sample at each station;

(2) summing the fines loads for all of the concurrent samples for a given station and water year to determine the cumulative fines load for concurrent samples for a given year;

(3) summing the suspended-sediment loads for all of the concurrent samples for a given station and water year to determine the cumulative suspended-sediment load for concurrent samples for a given year;

(4) dividing the cumulative fines load for the concurrent samples for a given station and water year by the cumulative suspended-sediment load to determine the percentage of fines in the cumulative loads for concurrent samples; and

(5) subtracting the percentage of fines in the cumulative loads from 100 percent to determine the percentage of sand in the cumulative loads for concurrent samples for a given station and water year

[2]The particle-size composition (percent fines and sand) of the cumulative annual suspended-sediment load for concurrent periodic water-quality samples was applied to the estimated annual suspended-sediment loads (table 6) to estimate the annual loads of fines and sand.

[3]Mass balance is the difference (net gain or loss) between the combined inflow to the main-stem reach and the outflow transported from the main-stem reach, as represented by Clark Fork at St. Regis, Mont. (station 12354500). Thus, a net gain (+) indicates net deposition in the reach and a net loss (–) indicates net removal from the reach.

to transport fines through the main-stem reach, but likely were not sufficient to transport all of the sand and resulted in a net gain of about 70,000 tons of suspended sediment in the main-stem reach during water year 2007. During water year 2008, streamflow at Clark Fork at St. Regis was above normal (table 3), but as in water year 2007, the suspended sediment in the combined inflow to the main-stem reach was predominantly sand (62.4 percent), and the suspended sediment in the outflow from the main-stem reach was predominantly fines (55.8 percent, fig. 15). There was an estimated net loss of fines (about 75,000 tons) from the main-stem reach, but a large net gain (deposition) of sand (about 146,000 tons) in the main-stem reach (table 7). The relatively large hydraulic energy in the Clark Fork during water year 2008 transported much more sand through the reach in water year 2008 than in water year 2007. However, because of the substantial amounts of sand transported into the reach after the breach of Milltown Dam, there was still a net gain (deposition) of about 71,000 tons of suspended sediment in the main-stem reach. During water year 2009, streamflow at Clark Fork at St. Regis (table 3) was above normal and suspended sediment in the combined gaged inflow to the main-stem reach was 50.4-percent fines, and the suspended sediment in the outflow from the main-stem reach was 52.0-percent fines (fig. 15). Thus, in water year 2009, the suspended sediment in the combined inflow to the main-stem reach had about equal percentages of fines and sand, but the suspended sediment in the outflow from the main-stem reach had the largest percentage of sand (48.0 percent) of any year (fig. 15). There was an estimated net loss of fines (about 108,000 tons) and sand (about 88,000 tons) from the main-stem reach in water year 2009, for a net loss of 196,000 tons of suspended sediment in the reach.

Another factor probably contributes to the occurrence and magnitude of net gains (deposition) of suspended sediment in the main-stem reach during water years 2007 and 2008. The increased hydraulic energies in the Clark Fork upstream from the Clark Fork above Missoula that resulted from the lowering of the water-surface elevation during permanent drawdown and the breach of Milltown Dam scoured substantial amounts of relatively coarse bottom sediments from the project area and transported them in suspension. Downstream from the project area outflow, the additional hydraulic energies associated with the lowering of the water-surface elevation in the project area probably subsided to levels typical of long-term conditions at similar streamflow magnitudes. The relatively lower hydraulic energies downstream from the project area outflow might not have been sufficient to maintain in suspension all of the coarse material scoured from the project area. However, some of the coarse material might have been transported as bedload below the unsampled zone of the water-quality samplers. An increase in bedload transport relative to suspended transport in the Clark Fork downstream from the project area outflow would contribute to the magnitude of calculated net gains of suspended sediment in the main-stem reach. However, because bedload data were not collected, it is

not possible to determine the effect of bedload transport on the net gain estimates.

Temporal variability in the relative contributions of estimated annual copper loads from source areas to the lower Clark Fork downstream from the project area outflow generally was similar to that of estimated annual suspended-sediment loads. During the years of the most substantial remediation activities (water years 2007 and 2008), the estimated annual loads for the project area outflow at Clark Fork above Missoula accounted for a large percentage (87 percent for water years 2007 and 2008) of the estimated annual copper load transported past the lower Clark Fork outflow. During water years 2006 and 2009 (before and after the most substantial remediation activities), the Clark Fork above Missoula accounted for a smaller percentage (60 percent for water year 2006 and 78 percent for water year 2009) of the estimated annual copper load transported past the lower Clark Fork outflow than in water years 2007 and 2008.

Annual net gains and losses of copper in the main-stem reach of the lower Clark Fork during water years 2006–09 varied in a pattern generally similar to those of suspended sediment, except during water year 2008 (fig. 14). During water year 2008, there was a large net gain (deposition) of suspended sediment in the main-stem reach, but there was a net loss of copper (fig. 14). Given the generally strong association between suspended-sediment transport and copper transport, it appears inconsistent that there would be net gains of suspended sediment in the main-stem reach in water year 2008 but net losses of copper. However, copper (and other metallic trace elements) tends to be more strongly associated with fine suspended sediment (fines) than with coarse suspended sediment (sand) (Horowitz, 1991). For example, for the nine periodic water-quality samples collected at Clark Fork at St. Regis during water year 2008 that had suspended sediment with percent fines greater than the median percent fines (76 percent) during water years 2006–09, the average solid-phase copper concentration of the suspended sediment was 1,290 µg/g. For the six periodic water-quality samples collected during water year 2008 that had suspended sediment with percent fines less than the median percent fines during water years 2006–09, the average solid-phase copper concentration of the suspended sediment was 162 µg/g. Thus, during water year 2008, solid-phase copper concentrations in samples with a greater than median proportion of fines were about 7 times larger than in the samples with a less than median proportion of fines. During water year 2008, there was an estimated net deposition in the main-stem reach of 146,000 tons of sand and an estimated net loss of 75,000 tons of fines, resulting in a net gain of 71,000 tons of suspended sediment (table 7). Although there was an overall net gain of suspended sediment in the main-stem reach, there actually was a net loss of fine sediment resulting in a corresponding net loss of copper, which is predominantly associated with fine sediment.

Temporal variability in the relative contributions of estimated annual arsenic loads from source areas to the lower Clark Fork downstream from the project area outflow differed somewhat from those of estimated annual suspended-sediment and copper loads, primarily because a relatively large proportion of arsenic is transported in dissolved phase in the Clark Fork. The project area outflow at Clark Fork above Missoula contributes about 50 percent or more of the annual arsenic load transported past the lower Clark Fork outflow for all years during 2006–09 (fig. 14). A substantial part of the arsenic load transported past the Clark Fork above Missoula was contributed from the basin upstream from Clark Fork at Turah Bridge in all years (fig. 12). There was large temporal variability in the contribution of arsenic from within the project area to the outflow at Clark Fork above Missoula. During the years of the most substantial remediation activities (water years 2007 and 2008), the project area accounted for a substantial percentage (about 36 percent for water year 2007 and about 48 percent for water year 2008; fig. 12) of the estimated annual arsenic load transported past Clark Fork above Missoula. During water years 2006 and 2009 (before and after the most substantial remediation activities), the project area accounted for a smaller percentage (8 percent for water year 2006 and 20 percent for water year 2009; fig. 12) of the estimated annual arsenic load transported past the Clark Fork above Missoula than in water years 2007–08. Even though the percent contribution of arsenic from within the project area was smaller during water year 2009 than during water years 2007 and 2008, the percent contribution of arsenic from the project area outflow at Clark Fork above Missoula to the lower Clark Fork was larger during water year 2009 than during any other year (fig. 14). The percent contribution of streamflow from the Clark Fork above Missoula to the lower Clark Fork also was larger during water year 2009 than during any other year. Arsenic generally occurs in dissolved phase in the Clark Fork and is readily transported downstream. Thus, the relatively larger arsenic load contributed from the project area outflow at Clark Fork above Missoula to the lower Clark Fork during water year 2009 probably is primarily attributable to the relatively larger streamflow contribution.

Annual net gains and losses of arsenic in the main-stem reach of the lower Clark Fork during water years 2006–09 varied in a pattern generally similar to those of copper. There were net losses of arsenic and copper from the main-stem reach during water years 2006, 2008, and 2009, and net gains of arsenic and copper in the main-stem reach during water year 2007. Although there were net gains for arsenic and copper in the main-stem reach during water year 2007, the percentage of the net gains in the reach relative to the combined gaged inflow to the reach were somewhat different between arsenic and copper. For arsenic in water year 2007, the net gain in the reach was 11 percent of the combined gaged inflow to the reach. For copper in water year 2007, the net gain in the reach was 31 percent of the combined gaged inflow to the reach. The smaller percentage of net gain for arsenic than for copper is attributable to the typically greater proportion of arsenic that occurs in dissolved phase and is readily transported downstream.

For all years, loads of all constituents contributed from the basin upstream from Flathead River at Perma to the lower Clark Fork outflow generally were small even though the Flathead River accounted for an average of 62 percent of the annual streamflow of the lower Clark Fork outflow. The interannual range in the percent contribution of estimated annual loads from the Flathead River at Perma to the lower Clark Fork outflow was 5 to 19 percent for suspended sediment, 4 to 11 percent for copper, and 17 to 26 percent for arsenic.

Summary and Conclusions

Milltown Reservoir is a National Priorities List Superfund site in the upper Clark Fork basin of western Montana where sediments enriched in trace elements from historical mining and ore processing have been deposited since the completion of Milltown Dam in 1908. Milltown Dam was breached on March 28, 2008, as part of Superfund remediation activities to remove the dam and excavate contaminated sediment that had accumulated in Milltown Reservoir. In preparation for the breach of Milltown Dam, permanent drawdown of Milltown Reservoir began on June 1, 2006, and lowered the water-surface elevation by about 10 to 12 ft. After the breach of Milltown dam, the water-surface elevation was lowered an additional 17 ft.

Hydrologic data-collection activities were conducted by the U.S. Geological Survey in cooperation with U.S. Environmental Protection Agency to estimate loads of suspended sediment and trace elements transported through the Clark Fork basin before and after the breach of Milltown Dam. High-intensity sampling was conducted at three stations that bracket the Milltown Reservoir project area. Daily and annual loads of suspended sediment and selected trace elements transported during water year 2009 were estimated for the three high-intensity stations and were used to quantify the net gain or loss (mass balance) of suspended sediment and trace elements within the project area for water year 2009. Estimated loads and mass balance within the project area for water year 2009 were compared to estimated loads and mass balance within the project area for selected periods before and after the breach of Milltown Dam, including (1) long-term average annual values for water years 1985–2005 (representing long-term average conditions during the period before the start of permanent drawdown of Milltown on June 1, 2006); (2) average annual values for 1996–97 (representing high-streamflow conditions during the period before the start of permanent drawdown of Milltown on June 1, 2006); (3) water years 2006–07 (representing the period between the start of permanent drawdown of Milltown Reservoir and the breach of Milltown Dam); and (4) water year 2008, during which Milltown Dam was breached.

Although this study primarily focused on the transport of suspended-sediment and trace-element loads to and from the project area, low-intensity sampling also was conducted during water years 2006–09 at four other stations. One low-intensity station was located within the Milltown Reservoir project area to provide information on erosional processes that occurred as the river adjusted to the steeper channel gradient caused by the breach of Milltown Dam; this site was sampled during water years 2008–09. Three low-intensity stations were located in the Clark Fork basin downstream from the project area outflow to provide general information on the transport of suspended-sediment and trace-element loads to and from reaches of the Clark Fork between the project area outflow and just downstream from the confluence with the Flathead River; these sites were sampled during water years 2006–09. Loads of suspended sediment and selected trace elements transported during water years 2006–09 were estimated for the three low-intensity stations in the lower Clark Fork and were used to evaluate how project area outflow loads were integrated into downstream transport processes.

For the high-intensity stations, daily loads of suspended sediment were estimated by using high-frequency sampling of the daily sediment monitoring. For the low-intensity stations, suspended-sediment loads were estimated by using regression equations relating suspended-sediment discharge to stream-flow. For all stations, daily loads of unfiltered-recoverable cadmium, copper, iron, lead, manganese, zinc, and arsenic were estimated by using regression equations relating trace-element discharge to either streamflow or suspended-sediment discharge. Regression equations for estimating constituent loads for water year 2009 were developed from instantaneous streamflow and concentration data for periodic water-quality samples collected during all or part of water years 2004–09. For some stations, there was substantial temporal variability in constituent transport relations. Thus, for some stations, the data were segregated into hydrologically based periods with similar transport relations and separate equations were developed.

All the regression equations used to estimate suspended-sediment and trace-element loads were statistically significant (p-values ranging <0.001 to 0.003). Regression equations for estimating water year 2009 trace-element discharge for the high-intensity stations have large R^2 values (average 0.97 and ranging from 0.94 to 1.00) and small SE values (average 22.8 percent and ranging from 11.4 to 36.3 percent) indicating good transport relations for all the trace elements at all three high-intensity stations. Regression equations for estimating water years 2006–09 suspended-sediment discharge for the low-intensity stations have moderate R^2 values (average 0.92 and ranging from 0.81 to 0.98) and generally moderate SE values (average 46.7 percent and ranging from 17.6 to 76.1 percent). Regression equations for estimating water years 2006–09 trace-element discharge for the low-intensity stations have moderate R^2 values (average 0.88 and ranging from 0.40 to 0.99) and generally moderate SE values (average 39.1 percent and ranging from 7.6 to 101.1 percent). Thus, the regression equations for estimating constituent discharge for the low-intensity stations indicate reasonably accurate transport relations. The SEs of the regression equations for the low-intensity stations generally are substantially larger than for the high-intensity stations and indicate lower confidence in the trace-element load estimates for the low-intensity stations than for the high-intensity stations. Thus, for the low-intensity stations, emphasis generally is placed on relative comparison of constituent load estimates between stations and between years, rather than on the absolute magnitude of load estimates. The regression equations were applied to records of daily mean streamflow or daily suspended-sediment loads to estimate daily trace-element loads.

Estimates of daily loads for the high-intensity stations were used to evaluate constituent transport to and from the project area for selected periods before and after the breach of Milltown Dam. Variations in estimated daily suspended-sediment loads transported to and from the project area during the period before the start of permanent drawdown generally coincided with variations in streamflow. For most of the period, streamflows generally were below normal, and differences between the suspended-sediment loads transported to and from the project area generally were minor (indicating approximate net balance) or indicated small amounts of deposition or scour. Consistent net loss of suspended sediment from the project area began with the start of permanent drawdown on June 1, 2006, and continued through the end of the drawdown period marked by the breach of Milltown Dam on March 28, 2008. During the permanent drawdown period, streamflow generally was below normal, but the pattern of near-continuous net loss of suspended sediment persisted for all streamflow conditions, and, at times, the loss of sediment from the project area was substantial. During water year 2008, after the breach of Milltown Dam, net loss of suspended sediment from the project area was substantially greater than during the permanent drawdown period because of generally above-normal streamflow and the steeper gradient that contributed to increased erosion. The outflow of suspended sediment from the project area sharply increased immediately after the breach of Milltown Dam resulting in large daily net losses. The large post-breach net losses of suspended sediment from the project area continued through the rising limb and peak flow of water year 2008. Net losses of suspended sediment began to decrease after the peak flow, reaching an approximate net balance between inflow and outflow loads by mid-August 2008. During the water year 2009 runoff period when streamflows generally were above normal, net losses increased substantially; the cumulative net loss during the runoff period was about 70,500 tons of sediment for an average of about 500 tons per day. Average streamflow for Clark Fork above Missoula during the water year 2009 runoff period was 6,400 ft³/s. In comparison, during the water year 2008 runoff period, the cumulative net loss was about 375,000 tons of sediment for an average of about 2,420 tons per day, and the average streamflow at Clark Fork above Missoula was about 5,430 ft³/s. After the water year 2009 runoff period, net losses decreased to about net balance conditions until the end of water year 2009. Although there were substantial net losses of suspended sediment from the project area during the water year 2009 runoff period, the losses were much smaller than during the water year 2008 runoff period, even though stream-flows were higher in water year 2009 than in water year 2008. Thus, there was substantial depletion of erodible channel materials in the project area by the end of water year 2008.

Variations in daily trace-element loads entering and leaving the project area generally coincided with variations in streamflow and suspended-sediment loads. The specific temporal variability in daily suspended-sediment loads and associated causal factors previously noted generally apply to variability in daily trace-element loads; copper and arsenic results are described as representative examples of trace-element transport characteristics. In early water year 2009, there was an approximate net balance between inflow and outflow loads within the project area for copper and arsenic. During the water year 2009 runoff period, net losses of copper and arsenic increased substantially. The cumulative net losses during the runoff period were about 25.5 tons of copper (average of about 0.181 ton per day) and about 3.1 tons of arsenic (average of about 0.022 ton per day). In comparison, during the water year 2008 runoff period, the cumulative net losses were about 150 tons of copper (average of about 0.971 ton per day) and about 11.6 tons of arsenic (average of about 0.075 ton per day).

Annual loads and mass balances for selected periods during water years 1985–2009 before and after the breach of Milltown Dam provide perspective on the effects of the hydro-logic conditions and activities associated with the removal of Milltown Dam. During the pre-drawdown period (water years 1985–2005) when Milltown Reservoir was operated as "run-of-the-river," there was an average annual net gain of suspended sediment (5,750 tons) in the project area, but relatively substantial average annual net loss (53,500 tons) during the above average (156 percent of long-term mean annual streamflow) streamflow years of 1996–97. When the "run-of-the-river" equilibrium was altered by the start of per-manent drawdown in June 2006, net losses of sediment from the project area increased immediately. In water year 2007 (the first full water year after the start of permanent draw-down), the annual contribution of suspended sediment from within the project area (130,000 tons) during below-average (84 percent) streamflow conditions was about 2.4 times larger than the average annual contribution (53,500 tons) from within the project area during the high-flow years 1996–97. Further, water year 2007 was the first water year that the contribution of suspended sediment from within the project area to the outflow was larger than the combined contributions from the two upstream source areas represented by the basins upstream from Clark Fork at Turah Bridge and Blackfoot River near Bonner. The breach of Milltown Dam further altered the project area environment and resulted in a large increase in net losses of suspended sediment from the project area.

The annual contribution of suspended sediment from within the project area during water year 2008 (391,000 tons) was the largest of any year in the monitoring period (77 percent of the outflow load) and occurred during slightly above-average (105 percent) streamflow conditions. However, the annual contribution of suspended sediment from within the project area during water year 2009 (76,200 tons) was substantially smaller than those in water years 2007 and 2008, even though streamflow was larger (122 percent of average) in water year 2009 than in water years 2007 and 2008. Thus, there was substantial depletion of the project area sediment supply by the end of water year 2008.

Interannual variability in copper transport was similar to interannual variability in suspended sediment transport. In water year 2007, the contribution of copper from within the project area (37.0 tons) was about 5.5 times larger than the average annual contribution during 1996–97 (6.75 tons). The annual contribution of copper from within the project area during water year 2008 (157 tons) was the largest of any year during the monitoring period (84 percent of the outflow load). The annual contribution of copper from within the project area during water year 2009 (29.0 tons) was smaller than during water years 2007 and 2008 even though streamflow was larger.

There were distinct differences in temporal variability of both total outflow loads from the project area and rela-tive contributions from source areas for arsenic compared to suspended sediment and copper. The basin upstream from Clark Fork at Turah Bridge accounted for the largest percent contribution of arsenic to the project area outflow from any upstream source area for all water years except 2008. For all water years, contributions of arsenic from within the project area were smaller than the combined contributions from the two upstream source areas represented by the basins upstream from Clark Fork at Turah Bridge and Blackfoot River near Bonner. Differences in the patterns of load contributions for arsenic relative to the other trace elements probably are attributable to the greater percentage of arsenic that occurs in dissolved phase relative to the other trace elements in the Clark Fork. Thus, the relatively small percentage of arsenic in particulate phase could have resulted in less historical deposition within the project area, and a smaller percentage of arsenic contributed from within the project area relative to the other trace elements. The annual contribution of arsenic from within the project area during water year 2009 (4.27 tons) was smaller than during water years 2007 and 2008 (6.10 and 13.2 tons, respectively). The relative reduction in the contribu-tion of arsenic from within the project area between water year 2008 and water year 2009 was substantial, but not as large as other trace elements.

Cumulative loads of constituents contributed from within the project area during the period June 1, 2006, to the end of water year 2009 provide perspective on the timing and effect of runoff or remediation activities associated with the removal of Milltown Dam on constituent transport from the project area. During this period, the estimated cumulative loads of suspended sediment, copper, and arsenic contributed from within the project area were 623,000 tons, 235 tons, and 26.8 tons, respectively. During the years of the most sub-stantial remediation activities (that is, water year 2007, when permanent drawdown was conducted for the entire year, and water year 2008 when Milltown Dam was breached) constituent loads relative to streamflow were proportionately larger than other years, and the relative contributions of constituents from within the project area also were larger than other years. The relative contributions of constituents from source areas during water years 2006 and 2009 (before and after the most substantial remediation activities) generally were similar. Thus, in a relatively short time frame after the start of the most substantial remediation activities (that is, the period from the start of permanent drawdown on June 1, 2006, to the end of water year 2008, during which two complete annual runoff periods occurred), constituent transport characteristics in the Clark Fork near the project area appear to be approaching typical conditions observed before the breach of Milltown Dam. However, remediation and restoration activities that occur after the end of water year 2009 might affect the apparent temporal pattern in constituent transport characteristics, for example, the diversion of the Clark Fork from the constructed bypass channel to a new channel that occurred in December 2010. Adjustment of the Clark Fork to a new geomorphic environment might alter patterns in constituent transport characteristics.

Estimated loads of suspended sediment and trace elements for water years 2006–09 at the three low-intensity stations located in the Clark Fork basin downstream from the project area outflow provide general information on constituent transport characteristics in the lower Clark Fork. Primary objectives for the investigation of constituent transport characteristics in the lower Clark Fork include (1) estimating the annual loads and source-area contributions to the Clark Fork downstream from the confluence with the Flathead River (the lower Clark Fork outflow), and (2) determining the mass balance of suspended-sediment and trace-element loads for an extensive main-stem reach (about 87 mi long) of the Clark Fork between the project area outflow at Clark Fork above Missoula and the Clark Fork at St. Regis.

Mass balance of constituent loads within the 87-mi main-stem reach of the Clark Fork between Clark Fork above Missoula and Clark Fork at St. Regis was determined as the difference between the combined annual inflow of the two gaged upstream source areas (that is, Clark Fork above Missoula and the Bitterroot River near Missoula) and the reach outflow (Clark Fork at St. Regis) for water years 2006–09. It is notable that there are somewhat substantial tributary inputs (about 18 percent of the drainage area and about 26 percent of the mean annual discharge) to the reach that were not gaged or monitored for water quality. Thus, the mass-balance calculations for the main-stem reach reflect an incomplete accounting of the interaction between net gains or losses of constituents within the Clark Fork channel and the undetermined contribution from ungaged tributary source areas. As a result, detailed determination of the fate of materials contributed from the project area outflow to the reach is not possible. However, the mass-balance calculations for the main-stem reach provide general information on temporal variability in constituent

transport in the reach and relative contributions from the two gaged source areas.

The effects of the Milltown Dam removal activities are apparent in the temporal variability in relative contributions of estimated annual suspended-sediment loads from source areas to the lower Clark Fork. During the years of the most substantial remediation activities (that is, water year 2007, when permanent drawdown was conducted for the entire year, and water year 2008, when Milltown Dam was breached), the estimated annual loads for the Clark Fork above Missoula (project area outflow) accounted for a large percentage (65 percent for water year 2007 and 70 percent for water year 2008) of the suspended-sediment load transported past the lower Clark Fork outflow. During water years 2006 and 2009 (before and after the most substantial remediation activities), the Clark Fork above Missoula accounted for smaller percentages (25 percent for water year 2006 and 38 percent for water year 2009) of the suspended-sediment load transported past the lower Clark Fork outflow than in water years 2007–08. Also, the relative contributions of suspended sediment from source areas during water years 2006 and 2009 generally were similar. Thus, in a relatively short time frame after the start of the most substantial remediation activities (that is, the period from the start of permanent drawdown on June 1, 2006, to the end of water year 2008, during which two complete annual runoff periods occurred), relative contributions of suspended sediment from upstream source areas to the lower Clark Fork appear to be approaching typical conditions observed before the breach of Milltown Dam. However, remediation and restoration activities that occur after the end of water year 2009 might affect the apparent temporal pattern in source-area contributions of suspended sediment to the lower Clark Fork. Adjustment of the Clark Fork to a new geomorphic environment might alter patterns in source-area contributions of suspended sediment to the lower Clark Fork.

The remediation activities associated with the removal of Milltown Dam affected the particle-size composition of suspended sediment transported through the lower Clark Fork and the mass balance of sediment in the main-stem reach. During the years of the most substantial remediation activities (water years 2007 and 2008), suspended sediment in periodic water-quality samples collected from the combined inflow to the main-stem reach was composed of predominantly sand (64.5 and 62.4 percent during water years 2007 and 2008, respectively), and suspended sediment in the outflow from the reach was composed of predominantly fines (61.6 and 55.8 percent during water years 2007 and 2008, respectively). The relatively large amounts of sand in the inflow resulted in a net gain of suspended sediment in the main-stem reach during water years 2007 and 2008. During the years before and after the most substantial remediation activities, suspended sediment in the inflow to and the outflow from the main-stem reach consisted of generally similar percentages of sand and fines. During water years 2006 and 2009, there were net losses of suspended sediment from the main-stem reach.

Temporal variability in the relative contributions of estimated annual copper loads from source areas to the lower Clark Fork downstream from the project area outflow generally was similar to that of estimated annual suspended-sediment loads. During the years of the most substantial remediation activities (water years 2007 and 2008), the estimated annual loads for the project area outflow at Clark Fork above Missoula accounted for a large percentage (87 percent for water years 2007 and 2008) of the estimated annual copper load transported past the lower Clark Fork outflow. During water years 2006 and 2009 (before and after the most substantial remediation activities), the Clark Fork above Missoula accounted for a smaller percentage (60 percent for water year 2006 and 78 percent for water year 2009) of the estimated annual copper load transported past the lower Clark Fork outflow than in water years 2007–08.

Annual net gains and losses of copper in the main-stem reach of the lower Clark Fork during water years 2006–09 varied in a pattern generally similar to those of suspended sediment, except during water year 2008. During water year 2008, there was a large net gain (deposition) of suspended sediment in the main-stem reach, but there was a net loss of copper. Although there was an overall net gain of suspended sediment in the main-stem reach, there actually was a net loss of fine sediment resulting in a corresponding net loss of copper, which is predominantly associated with fine sediment.

Temporal variability in the relative contributions of estimated annual arsenic loads from source areas to the lower Clark Fork downstream from the project area outflow differed somewhat from those of estimated annual suspended-sediment and copper loads, primarily because a relatively large proportion of arsenic is transported in dissolved phase in the Clark Fork. The project area outflow at Clark Fork above Missoula contributes about 50 percent or more of the arsenic load transported past the lower Clark Fork outflow for all years during 2006–09. A substantial part of the arsenic load transported past the Clark Fork above Missoula was contributed from the basin upstream from Clark Fork at Turah Bridge in all years.

Annual net gains and losses of arsenic in the main-stem reach of the lower Clark Fork during water years 2006–09 varied in a pattern generally similar to those of copper. There were net losses of arsenic and copper from the main-stem reach during water years 2006, 2008, and 2009, and net gains of arsenic and copper in the main-stem reach during water year 2007.

For all years, loads of all constituents contributed from the basin upstream from Flathead River at Perma to the lower Clark Fork outflow generally were small even though the Flathead River accounted for an average of 62 percent of the annual streamflow of the lower Clark Fork outflow. The inter-annual range in the percent contribution of estimated annual loads from the Flathead River at Perma to the lower Clark Fork outflow was 5 to 19 percent for suspended sediment, 4 to 11 percent for copper, and 17 to 26 percent for arsenic.

Acknowledgments

Special thanks are given to Russ Forba (retired), Kristine Edwards, and Diana Hammer of the USEPA for their support of this study. Special thanks also are given to Bill Bakeberg and Michael Kriesberg for their diligent efforts in collecting high-frequency suspended-sediment samples. Technical reviews by Jill Frankforter and Galen Hoogestraat improved the report and are greatly appreciated. Finally, special thanks are given to the dedicated hydrologic technicians and hydrologists of the USGS who collected the streamflow and water-quality data for this study; notable individuals include Kent A. Dodge, Terry L. Heinert, Craig L. Bowers, Rod R. Caldwell, Thomas E. Cleasby, Wayne A. Tice, and Allen L. Furlow.

References Cited

Cleveland, W.S., 1985, The elements of graphing data: Monterey, Calif., Wadsworth Books, 323 p.

Cleveland, W.S., and McGill, R., 1984, The many faces of a scatterplot: Journal of the American Statistical Association, v. 79, p. 807–822.

Cohn, T.A., Caulder, D.L., Gilroy, E.J., Zynjuk, L.D., and Sommers, R.M., 1992, The validity of a simple statistical model for estimating fluvial constituent loads—An empirical study involving nutrient loads entering Chesapeake Bay: Water Resources Research, v. 28, p. 2352–2363.

Colby, B.R., 1956, Relationship of sediment discharge to streamflow: U.S. Geological Survey Open-File Report 56–27, 170 p.

Dodge, K.A., Hornberger, M.I., and Dyke, J.L., 2009, Water-quality, bed-sediment, and biological data (October 2007 through September 2008) and statistical summaries of long-term data for streams in the Clark Fork basin, Montana: U.S. Geological Survey Open-File Report 2009–1178, 139 p., accessed October 29, 2010, at *http://pubs.usgs.gov/of/2009/1178/*.

Dodge, K.A., Hornberger, M.I., and Dyke, J.L., 2010, Water-quality, bed-sediment, and biological data (October 2008 through September 2009) and statistical summaries of long-term data for streams in the Clark Fork basin, Montana: U.S. Geological Survey Open-File Report 2010–1267, 137 p.

Dodge, K.A., and Lambing, J.H., 2006, Quality-assurance plan for the analysis of suspended sediment by the U.S. Geological Survey in Montana: U.S. Geological Survey Open-File Report 2006–1242, 25 p., accessed October 29, 2010, at *http://pubs.water.usgs.gov/ofr2006-1242.*

Duan, N., 1983, A nonparametric retransformation method: Journal of the American Statistical Association, v. 78, no. 383, p. 605–610.

Edwards, T.K., and Glysson, G.D., 1999, Field methods for measurement of fluvial sediment: U.S. Geological Survey Techniques of Water-Resources Investigations, book 3, chap. C2, 89 p., accessed October 29, 2010, at *http://pubs.water.usgs.gov/twri/*.

Friedman, L.C., and Erdmann, D.E., 1982, Quality assurance practices for the chemical and biological analyses of water and fluvial sediments: U.S. Geological Survey Techniques of Water-Resources Investigations, book 5, chap. A6, 181 p., accessed October 29, 2010, at *http://pubs.water.usgs.gov/twri/*.

Garbarino, J.R., and Struzeski, T.M., 1998, Methods of analysis by the U.S. Geological Survey National Water Quality Laboratory—Determination of elements in whole-water digests using inductively coupled plasma–optical emission spectrometry and inductively coupled plasma–mass spectrometry: U.S. Geological Survey Open-File Report 98–165, 101 p.

Guy, H.P., 1969, Laboratory theory and methods for sediment analysis: U.S. Geological Survey Techniques of Water-Resources Investigations, book 5, chap. C1, 58 p., accessed October 29, 2010, at *http://pubs.water.usgs.gov/twri/*.

Helsel, D.R., 2005, Nondetects and data analysis—Statistics for censored environmental data: Hoboken, N.J., Wiley-Interscience, 250 p.

Helsel, D.R., and Hirsch, R.M., 2002, Statistical methods in water resources: U.S. Geological Survey Techniques of Water-Resources Investigations, book 4, chap. A3, 524 p., accessed October 29, 2010, at *http://pubs.water.usgs.gov/twri/twri4a3/*.

Hoffman, G.L., Fishman, M.J., and Garbarino, J.R., 1996, Methods of analysis by the U.S. Geological Survey National Water Quality Laboratory—In-bottle digestion of whole-water samples: U.S. Geological Survey Open-File Report 96–225, 28 p.

Hornberger, M.I., Lambing, J.H., Luoma, S.N., and Axtmann, E.V., 1997, Spatial and temporal trends of trace metals in surface water, bed sediment, and biota of the upper Clark Fork basin, Montana, 1985–95: U.S. Geological Survey Open-File Report 97–669, 127 p.

Horowitz, A.J., 1991, A primer on sediment-trace element chemistry (2nd ed.): Chelsea, Mich., Lewis Publishers, Inc., 136 p.

Horowitz, A.J., Demas, C.R., Fitzgerald, K.K., Miller, T.L., and Rickert, D.A., 1994, U.S. Geological Survey protocol for the collection and processing of surface-water samples for the subsequent determination of inorganic constituents in filtered water: U.S. Geological Survey Open-File Report 97–669, 84 p.

Jones, B.E., 1987, Quality control manual of the U.S. Geological Survey's National Water Quality Laboratory: U.S. Geological Survey Open-File Report 87–457, 17 p.

Koch, R.W., and Smillie, G.M., 1986, Bias in hydrologic prediction using log-transformed regression models: Water Resources Bulletin, v. 22, p. 717–723.

Lambing, J.H., 1991, Water quality and transport characteristics of suspended sediment and trace elements in streamflow of the upper Clark Fork basin from Galen to Missoula, Montana, 1985–90: U.S. Geological Survey Water-Resources Investigations Report 91–4139, 73 p.

Lambing, J.H., 1998, Estimated 1996–97 and long-term average annual loads for suspended sediment and selected trace metals in streamflow of the upper Clark Fork basin from Warm Springs to Missoula, Montana: U.S. Geological Survey Water-Resources Investigations Report 98–4137, 35 p.

Lambing, J.H., comp., 2006, Quality-assurance plan for water-quality activities of the U.S. Geological Survey Montana Water Science Center: U.S. Geological Survey Open-File Report 2006–1275, 39 p., accessed October 29, 2010, at *http://pubs.usgs.gov/of/2006/1275*.

Lambing, J.H., and Sando, S.K., 2008, Estimated loads of suspended sediment and selected trace elements transported through Milltown Reservoir in the upper Clark Fork basin, Montana, water years 2004–07: U.S. Geological Survey Scientific Investigations Report 2008–5080, 24 p., accessed October 29, 2010, at *http://pubs.usgs.gov/sir/2008/5080*.

Lambing, J.H., and Sando, S.K., 2009, Estimated loads of suspended sediment and selected trace elements transported through Milltown Reservoir project area before and after the breaching of Milltown Dam in the upper Clark Fork basin, Montana, water year 2008: U.S. Geological Survey Scientific Investigations Report 2009–5095, 30 p., accessed October 29, 2010, at *http://pubs.usgs.gov/sir/2009/5095*.

Maloney, T.J., ed., 2005, Quality management system, U.S. Geological Survey National Water Quality Laboratory: U.S. Geological Survey Open-File Report 2005–1263, version 1.3, November 9, 2005, chapters and appendixes [variously paged], accessed October 29, 2010, at *http://pubs.usgs.gov/of/2005/1263/*.

Moore, J.N., Luoma, S.N., and Peters, Donald, 1991, Downstream effects of mine effluent on an intermontane riparian system: Canadian Journal of Fisheries and Aquatic Sciences, v. 48, p. 222–232.

Porterfield, George, 1972, Computation of fluvial-sediment discharge: U.S. Geological Survey Techniques of Water-Resources Investigations, book 3, chap. C3, 66 p., accessed October 29, 2010, at *http://pubs.usgs.gov/twri/twri3-c3/*.

Pritt, J.W., and Raese, J.W., 1995, Quality assurance/quality control manual, National Water Quality Laboratory: U.S. Geological Survey Open-File Report 95–443, 35 p.

Rantz, S.E., and others, 1982, Measurement and computation of streamflow (volumes 1 and 2): U.S. Geological Survey Water-Supply Paper 2175, 2 v., 631 p.

Taylor, J.K., 1987, Quality assurance of chemical measurements: Chelsea, Mich., Lewis Publishers, 328 p.

U.S. Environmental Protection Agency, 2004, Milltown Reservoir Sediments Operable Unit of the Milltown Reservoir/ Clark Fork River Superfund Site—Record of Decision, Part 2: U.S. Environmental Protection Agency Decision Summary, 141 p., accessed October 29, 2010, at *http://www. epa.gov/region8/superfund/mt/milltown/mrsrod.html*.

U.S. Geological Survey, variously dated, National field manual for the collection of water-quality data: U.S. Geological Survey Techniques of Water-Resources Investigations, book 9, chaps. A1–A9, accessed October 29, 2010, at *http:// pubs.water.usgs.gov/twri/*.

Ward, J.R., and Harr, C.A., eds., 1990, Methods for collection and processing of surface-water and bed-material samples for physical and chemical analyses: U.S. Geological Survey Open-File Report 90–140, 71 p.

White, M.K., Shields, R.R., and Dodge, K.A., 1998, Surface-water quality-assurance plan for the Montana District of the U.S. Geological Survey: U.S. Geological Survey Open-File Report 98–173, 54 p.

Supplement 1.   Methods for Estimating Censored Concentrations for Water Year 2009 and Comparison with Methods Used in Previous Years

In previous reports presenting estimated loads of trace elements for the high-intensity stations (Lambing, 1991; Lambing, 1998; Hornberger and others, 1997; Lambing and Sando, 2008, 2009), values for trace-element concentrations that were censored were estimated by substituting one-half of the RL (reporting limit) in effect during the data-collection period for purposes of plotting and analysis of statistical relations. For constituents that had multiple RLs during the data-collection period, one-half of the median RL during the period was substituted. Data analysis indicated that this approach for handling censored concentrations was suitable for meeting the study objectives (Lambing and Sando, 2009) and did not substantially bias the study results. However, load estimates for constituents having greater than about 30-percent censored concentrations for a given site were qualified as having greater uncertainty than constituents with no or a very small percent of censored concentrations.

A more rigorous method of estimating censored concentrations [Adjusted Maximum Likelihood Estimation (AMLE) regression; Helsel and Hirsch, 2002] was used in this report for water year 2009 data for the high-intensity stations and water years 2006–09 data for the low-intensity stations. Factors that contributed to the need for using AMLE regression include (1) the NWQL RL for unfiltered-recoverable copper (an important constituent in terms of potential toxicity and representation of constituent transport) increased substantially between water years 2008 and 2009 (from 1.2 to 4 mg/L), and (2) two of the low-intensity stations (Bitterroot River near Missoula and Flathead River at Perma) for which load estimates are presented in this report had relatively high proportions of censored concentrations of some trace elements (table 4). The increase in the NWQL RL for unfiltered-recoverable copper in water year 2009 resulted in greater uncertainty in estimating the copper load for Blackfoot River near Bonner, a critical inflow station for determining the annual mass balance in the Milltown Reservoir project area. For example, about 20 percent of unfiltered-recoverable copper concentrations for Blackfoot River near Bonner were censored during water years 2006–08, but about 60 percent of the concentrations were censored during water year 2009. The high-streamflow conditions of water year 2009 also have the potential to magnify the effect of uncertainty associated with censored concentrations on load estimates and estimating the annual mass balance of copper for the project area for water year 2009. Two low-intensity stations (Bitterroot River near Missoula and Flathead River at Perma) have relatively high percent censored concentrations for cadmium and copper (both stations) and zinc (Flathead River at Perma). Load estimates for these two stations are critical for evaluating trace-element transport characteristics for the Clark Fork basin downstream from the project area outflow. Reducing uncertainty in estimating loads for samples with censored concentrations improves

the accuracy of determining trace-element transport characteristics in the lower Clark Fork basin.

AMLE regression analyzes the relation between a given trace element with some censored concentrations (the response variable) and some other constituent (the explanatory variable) with all reported concentrations above the RL (no censored concentrations). The relation between the response and explanatory variables is determined using available sample pairs with reported concentrations above the RL for both the response and explanatory variables. Proportions of censored concentrations of the response variable for various reporting levels also are analyzed in relation to the associated explanatory-variable concentrations above the RL. These relations are used to determine equations that estimate the most likely values of the censored concentrations of the response variable based on the associated reported concentrations of the explanatory variable. For data sets of at least 50 uncensored sample pairs (which applies to all station and trace-element combinations with censored concentrations in this report), AMLE regression is the preferred method for estimating values of censored concentrations (Helsel, 2005).

Equations developed by using AMLE regression for each station and trace-element combination that had some censored concentrations (table 4) are presented in tables S1.1 and S1.2 for the high-intensity and low-intensity stations, respectively. To evaluate differences between results of the AMLE method and results of the substitution method, AMLE-estimated concentrations were compared to substitution-estimated concentrations for water year 2008 samples collected at Blackfoot River near Bonner. The average relative percent difference between the AMLE and substitution estimates were (1) 4 percent for 15 censored unfiltered-recoverable cadmium concentrations, (2) 8 percent for 8 censored unfiltered-recoverable copper concentrations, and (3) 10 percent for 8 censored unfiltered-recoverable zinc concentrations. The relative percent differences between the estimates of the two methods are relatively small.

Consideration of how the estimated censored concentrations are used to develop load estimates provides further perspective on the suitability of comparison of load estimates in this report with previously reported estimates to evaluate temporal variability in trace-element transport in the Clark Fork basin. The estimated censored concentrations are used in conjunction with the associated streamflow to calculate instantaneous trace-element discharges for the given periodic water-quality samples. Thus, variability in trace-element discharges among samples reflects variability in both constituent concentration and streamflow. Censored values generally are associated with low to moderate streamflows and do not substantially affect calculations of trace-element discharges for high-flow samples representative of typically higher (uncensored) concentrations and conditions when the largest

Table S1.1. Regression equations for estimating unfiltered-recoverable trace-element concentrations for censored data for the high-intensity data-collection stations (table 1), water year 2009.

[Abbreviations: N, number of values; p-value, significance level; SE, standard error of estimate, in percent; LOG, base 10 logarithm; AS, arsenic concentration, in micrograms per liter; CD, cadmium concentration, in micrograms per liter; SED, suspended-sediment concentration, in milligrams per liter; CU, copper concentration, in micrograms per liter; FE, iron concentration, in micrograms per liter; PB, lead concentration, in micrograms per liter; MN, manganese concentration, in micrograms per liter; ZN, zinc concentration, in micrograms per liter. Symbol: <, less than]

Trace element	Equation	N	p-value	SE
\multicolumn{5}{c}{Clark Fork at Turah Bridge near Bonner, Mont. (station 12334550)}				
\multicolumn{5}{c}{Equations applied to water year 2009. Equations developed using data collected water years 2004–09}				
Cadmium	$CD=0.00296(MN)^{0.871}$	103	<0.001	23.0
\multicolumn{5}{c}{Blackfoot River near Bonner, Mont. (station 12340000)}				
\multicolumn{5}{c}{Equations applied to water year 2009. Equations developed using data collected water years 2004–09}				
Cadmium	$CD=0.000367(FE)^{0.555}$	93	<0.001	65.7
Copper	$CU=0.200(MN)^{0.673}$	94	<.001	43.7
Lead	$PB=0.00123(FE)^{1.01}$	94	<.001	24.7
Zinc	$ZN=0.0508(FE)^{0.675}$	93	<.001	33.6
Arsenic	$LOG(AS)=0.0208(SED^{0.500})-0.00710$	94	<.001	21.5
\multicolumn{5}{c}{Clark Fork above Missoula, Mont. (station 12340500)}				
\multicolumn{5}{c}{Equations applied to water year 2009. Equations developed using data collected water years 2004–09}				
Cadmium	$CD=0.000629(FE)^{0.853}$	104	<0.001	47.5

Table S1.2. Regression equations for estimating unfiltered-recoverable trace-element concentrations for censored data for low-intensity data-collection stations (table 1) in the lower Clark Fork basin, water years 2006–09.

[Abbreviations: N, number of values; p-value, significance level; SE, standard error of estimate, in percent; LOG, base 10 logarithm; CD, cadmium concentration, in micrograms per liter; SED, suspended-sediment concentration, in milligrams per liter; CU, copper concentration, in micrograms per liter; FE, iron concentration, in micrograms per liter; PB, lead concentration, in micrograms per liter; MN, manganese concentration, in micrograms per liter; ZN, zinc concentration, in micrograms per liter. Symbol: <, less than]

Trace element	Equation	N	p-value	SE
\multicolumn{5}{c}{Bitterroot River near Missoula, Mont. (station 12352500)}				
\multicolumn{5}{c}{Equations applied to and developed using data collected during water years 2006–09}				
Cadmium	$CD=0.000437(FE)^{0.495}$	55	<0.001	59.9
Copper	$LOG(CU)=0.0588(SED^{0.500})-0.273$	55	<.001	21.7
Lead	$PB=0.000500(FE)^{1.10}$	55	<.001	19.1
Zinc	$ZN=0.0294(FE)^{0.730}$	54	<.001	50.9
\multicolumn{5}{c}{Clark Fork at St. Regis, Mont. (station 12354500)}				
\multicolumn{5}{c}{Equations applied to and developed using data collected during water years 2006–09}				
Cadmium	$CD=0.00116(MN)^{1.10}$	55	<0.001	50.1
\multicolumn{5}{c}{Flathead River near Perma, Mont.[1] (station 12388700)}				
\multicolumn{5}{c}{Equations applied to and developed using data collected during water years 2006–09}				
Copper	$CU=0.0505(MN)^{1.23}$	53	0.007	103
Lead	$PB=0.00137(FE)^{0.994}$	54	<.001	25.7
Zinc	$ZN=0.0178(FE)^{0.776}$	53	.005	85.9

[1]Flathead River at Perma had a very large percent (94.4 percent; table 4) of censored values for unfiltered-recoverable cadmium, which precluded the development of regression equations for estimating censored concentrations. No results are presented in this report for unfiltered-recoverable cadmium for Flathead River at Perma.

constituent transport occurs. Variability in trace-element concentrations generally is small during low to moderate streamflows relative to variability during higher streamflows. Further, the discharges for samples affected by censoring are combined with discharges for samples not affected by censoring (that is, with reported concentrations above the RL) to develop regression equations based on relations with explanatory variables. The regression equations are then used

to develop load estimates. Thus, although AMLE regression is the preferred method for estimating censored concentrations and provides the most accurate estimates for water year 2009 for the high-intensity stations and water years 2006–09 for the low-intensity stations, differences between results of the AMLE regression method and results of the substitution method generally are relatively small and do not substantially affect comparison of load estimates among water years.

Supplement 2. Regression Equations for Estimating Suspended-Sediment and Trace-Element Discharge for the High-Intensity Stations

Table S2.1. Regression equations for estimating unfiltered-recoverable trace-element discharge for Clark Fork at Turah Bridge, near Bonner, Mont. (station 12334550), water year 2009.

[Abbreviations: N, number of values; R^2, coefficient of determination; p-value, significance level; SE, standard error of estimate, in percent; RBCF, retransformation-bias-correction factor; CDQ, cadmium discharge, in tons per day; SEDQ, suspended-sediment discharge, in tons per day; CUQ, copper discharge, in tons per day; FEQ, iron discharge, in tons per day; PBQ, lead discharge, in tons per day; MNQ, manganese discharge, in tons per day; ZNQ, zinc discharge, in tons per day; ASQ, arsenic discharge, in tons per day; Q, streamflow, in cubic feet per second. Symbol: <, less than]

Trace element	Equation	N	R^2	p-value	SE	RBCF
Equations applied to all of water year 2009. Equations developed using data collected during water years 2004–09						
Cadmium	$CDQ=0.0000144(SEDQ)^{0.760}$	103	0.97	<0.001	22.3	1.00
Copper	$CUQ=0.00137(SEDQ)^{0.840}$	103	.97	<.001	25.2	1.01
Iron	$FEQ=0.0181(SEDQ)^{0.982}$	103	.99	<.001	20.6	1.00
Lead	$PBQ=0.000123(SEDQ)^{0.960}$	103	.97	<.001	29.7	1.01
Manganese	$MNQ=0.00637(SEDQ)^{0.813}$	103	.98	<.001	19.5	1.00
Zinc	$ZNQ=0.00177(SEDQ)^{0.858}$	103	.97	<.001	25.5	1.01
Arsenic	$ASQ=0.00000247(Q)^{1.28}$	103	.94	<.001	25.0	1.01

Table S2.2. Regression equations for estimating unfiltered-recoverable trace-element discharge for Blackfoot River near Bonner, Mont. (station 12340000), water year 2009.

[Abbreviations: N, number of values; R^2, coefficient of determination; p-value, significance level; SE, standard error of estimate, in percent; RBCF, retransformation-bias-correction factor; CDQ, cadmium discharge, in tons per day; SEDQ, suspended-sediment discharge, in tons per day; CUQ, copper discharge, in tons per day; FEQ, iron discharge, in tons per day; PBQ, lead discharge, in tons per day; MNQ, manganese discharge, in tons per day; ZNQ, zinc discharge, in tons per day; LOG, base 10 logarithm; ASQ, arsenic discharge, in tons per day; Q, streamflow, in cubic feet per second. Symbol: <, less than]

Trace element	Equation	N	R^2	p-value	SE	RBCF
Equations applied to all of water year 2009. Equations developed using data collected during water years 2004–09						
Cadmium	$CDQ=0.00000348(SEDQ)^{0.619}$	93	0.95	<0.001	35.1	1.01
Copper	$CUQ=0.000414(SEDQ)^{0.697}$	94	.95	<.001	36.3	1.01
Iron	$FEQ=0.0224(SEDQ)^{0.912}$	94	.99	<.001	26.1	1.01
Lead	$PBQ=0.0000282(SEDQ)^{0.926}$	94	.99	<.001	25.9	1.01
Manganese	$MNQ=0.00289(SEDQ)^{0.820}$	94	.98	<.001	24.1	1.01
Zinc	$ZNQ=0.000467(SEDQ)^{0.735}$	93	.97	<.001	28.2	1.01
Arsenic	$LOG(ASQ)=0.107(Q^{0.333})-3.59$	94	.97	<.001	18.7	1.00

Table S2.3.   Regression equations for estimating unfiltered-recoverable trace-element discharge for Clark Fork above Missoula, Mont. (station 12340500), water year 2009.

[Abbreviations: N, number of values; R^2, coefficient of determination; p-value, significance level; SE, standard error of estimate, in percent; RBCF, retransformation-bias-correction factor; CDQ, cadmium discharge, in tons per day; SEDQ, suspended-sediment discharge, in tons per day; CUQ, copper discharge, in tons per day; FEQ, iron discharge, in tons per day; PBQ, lead discharge, in tons per day; MNQ, manganese discharge, in tons per day; ZNQ, zinc discharge, in tons per day; LOG, base 10 logarithm; ASQ, arsenic discharge, in tons per day; Q, streamflow, in cubic feet per second. Symbol: <, less than]

Trace element	Equation	N	R^2	p-value	SE	RBCF
	Equations applied to the part of water year 2009 before the start of the rising limb of the runoff period (October 1, 2008–March 8, 2009) Equations developed using data collected May 23, 2008–March 8, 2009
Cadmium	$CDQ=0.00000850(SEDQ)^{0.829}$	11	0.99	<0.001	25.5	1.00
Copper	$CUQ=0.00138(SEDQ)^{0.823}$	11	.99	<.001	18.8	1.00
Iron	$FEQ=0.0256(SEDQ)^{0.888}$	11	1.00	<.001	11.4	1.00
Lead	$PBQ=0.000158(SEDQ)^{0.862}$	11	.98	<.001	34.5	1.01
Manganese	$MNQ=0.0139(SEDQ)^{0.663}$	11	.99	<.001	17.6	1.00
Zinc	$ZNQ=0.00167(SEDQ)^{0.863}$	11	.99	<.001	19.8	1.00
Arsenic	$LOG(ASQ)=0.103(Q^{0.333})-2.93$	11	.98	<.001	18.4	1.00
	Equations applied to and developed using data collected during the rising limb of the water year 2009 runoff period (March 9–June 1, 2009)
Cadmium	$CDQ=0.0000117(SEDQ)^{0.773}$	17	0.95	<0.001	28.7	1.01
Copper	$CUQ=0.00228(SEDQ)^{0.745}$	17	.96	<.001	25.1	1.01
Iron	$FEQ=0.0403(SEDQ)^{0.844}$	17	.99	<.001	16.3	1.00
Lead	$PBQ=0.000295(SEDQ)^{0.789}$	17	.97	<.001	21.7	1.00
Manganese	$MNQ=0.00665(SEDQ)^{0.766}$	17	.98	<.001	16.3	1.00
Zinc	$ZNQ=0.00272(SEDQ)^{0.779}$	17	.95	<.001	29.5	1.01
Arsenic	$ASQ=0.00193(SEDQ)^{0.568}$	17	.98	<.001	14.8	1.00
	Equations applied to and developed using data collected during the falling limb of the water year 2009 runoff period (June 2–September 30, 2009)
Cadmium	$CDQ=0.0000281(SEDQ)^{0.683}$	9	0.96	<0.001	24.7	1.00
Copper	$CUQ=0.00216(SEDQ)^{0.773}$	9	.97	<.001	24.5	1.00
Iron	$FEQ=0.0306(SEDQ)^{0.874}$	9	.99	<.001	15.4	1.00
Lead	$PBQ=0.000242(SEDQ)^{0.818}$	9	.98	<.001	21.3	1.00
Manganese	$MNQ=0.0142(SEDQ)^{0.680}$	9	.98	<.001	16.1	1.00
Zinc	$ZNQ=0.00193(SEDQ)^{0.850}$	9	.98	<.001	21.0	1.00
Arsenic	$LOG(ASQ)=0.0810(Q^{0.333})-2.50$	9	.97	<.001	13.7	1.00

Supplement 3.   Regression Equations for Estimating Suspended-Sediment and Trace-Element Discharge for the Low-Intensity Stations

Table S3.1.   Regression equations for estimating suspended-sediment and unfiltered-recoverable trace-element discharge for Bitterroot River near Missoula, Mont. (station 12352500), water years 2006–09.

[Abbreviations: N, number of values; R^2, coefficient of determination; p-value, significance level; SE, standard error of estimate, in percent; RBCF, retransformation-bias-correction factor; SEDQ, suspended-sediment discharge, in tons per day; Q, streamflow, in cubic feet per second; CDQ, cadmium discharge, in tons per day; LOG, base 10 logarithm; CUQ, copper discharge, in tons per day; FEQ, iron discharge, in tons per day; PBQ, lead discharge, in tons per day; MNQ, manganese discharge, in tons per day; ZNQ, zinc discharge, in tons per day; ASQ, arsenic discharge, in tons per day. Symbol: <, less than]

Constituent	Equation	N	R^2	p-value	SE	RBCF
Equations applied to and developed using data collected[1] during the rising limbs of water years 2006–09 runoff periods (March 21–May 21, 2006; March 3–May 14, 2007; March 9–May 21, 2008; March 9–June 1, 2009)						
Suspended sediment	$SEDQ=0.00000265(Q)^{2.27}$	29	0.92	<0.001	66.1	1.03
Cadmium	$CDQ=0.000000000548(Q)^{1.49}$	29	.91	<.001	44.9	1.02
Copper	$LOG(CUQ)=0.0214(Q^{0.500})-3.28$	29	.94	<.001	36.0	1.01
Iron	$FEQ=0.000000774(Q)^{1.92}$	29	.93	<.001	52.3	1.02
Lead	$PBQ=0.000000000465(Q)^{1.97}$	29	.93	<.001	52.6	1.02
Manganese	$MNQ=0.0181(Q)^{0.0187}$	29	.84	<.001	57.6	1.03
Zinc	$ZNQ=0.0000000855(Q)^{1.56}$	28	.85	<.001	66.3	1.03
Arsenic	$ASQ=0.000000427(Q)^{1.13}$	29	.95	<.001	23.5	1.00
Equations applied to and developed using data collected[1] during the falling limbs (and all other nonrising-limb periods) of water years 2006–09 (October 1, 2005–March 20, 2006; May 22, 2006–March 2, 2007; May 15, 2007–March 8, 2008; May 22, 2008–March 8, 2009; and June 2–September 30, 2009)						
Suspended sediment	$SEDQ=0.000000284(Q)^{2.41}$	26	0.98	<0.001	33.8	1.01
Cadmium	$CDQ=0.000000000618(Q)^{1.41}$	26	.98	<.001	19.1	1.00
Copper	$LOG(CUQ)=0.110(Q^{0.333})-3.79$	26	.97	<.001	20.7	1.00
Iron	$FEQ=0.000000768(Q)^{1.81}$	26	.99	<.001	18.5	1.00
Lead	$LOG(PBQ)=0.160(Q^{0.333})-5.35$	26	.98	<.001	23.3	1.00
Manganese	$LOG(MNQ)=0.114(Q0^{.333})-2.73$	26	.98	<.001	18.3	1.00
Zinc	$ZNQ=0.0000000358(Q)^{1.57}$	26	.96	<.001	26.3	1.01
Arsenic	$LOG(ASQ)=0.0790(Q^{0.333})-3.65$	26	.98	<.001	12.4	1.00

[1]In some cases, data collected immediately before or after the indicated period were included in the regression analyses if those data were determined to improve the regression relations.

Table S3.2. Regression equations for estimating suspended-sediment and unfiltered-recoverable trace-element discharge for Clark Fork at St. Regis, Mont. (station 12354500), water years 2006–09

[Abbreviations: N, number of values; R^2, coefficient of determination; p-value, significance level; SE, standard error of estimate, in percent; RBCF, retransformation-bias-correction factor; SEDQ, suspended-sediment discharge, in tons per day; Q, streamflow, in cubic feet per second; CDQ, cadmium discharge, in tons per day; CUQ, copper discharge, in tons per day; FEQ, iron discharge, in tons per day; PBQ, lead discharge, in tons per day; MNQ, manganese discharge, in tons per day; ZNQ, zinc discharge, in tons per day; ASQ, arsenic discharge, in tons per day; LOG, base 10 logarithm. Symbol: <, less than]

Constituent	Equation	N	R^2	p-value	SE	RBCF
Equations applied to and developed using data collected during the rising limbs of water years 2006–07 runoff periods (March 21–May 21, 2006; March 3–May 14, 2007)						
Suspended sediment	$SEDQ=0.00000000445(Q)^{2.79}$	11	0.81	<0.001	76.1	1.04
Cadmium	$CDQ=0.000000000424(Q)^{1.65}$	11	.67	.002	63.1	1.03
Copper	$CUQ=0.0000000613(Q)^{1.64}$	11	.66	.002	64.5	1.03
Iron	$FEQ=0.00000000486(Q)^{2.33}$	11	.76	.001	74.0	1.04
Lead	$PBQ=0.000000000804(Q)^{1.92}$	11	.70	.001	69.1	1.03
Manganese	$MNQ=0.000000181(Q)^{1.70}$	11	.65	.003	69.3	1.03
Zinc	$ZNQ=0.0000000747(Q)^{1.68}$	11	.64	.003	69.6	1.03
Arsenic	$ASQ=0.00000127(Q)^{1.18}$	11	.74	.001	36.3	1.01
Equations applied to and developed using data collected during the falling limbs (and all other nonrising-limb periods) of water years 2006–07 (October 1, 2005–March 20, 2006; May 22, 2006–March 2, 2007; May 15, 2007–September 30, 2007)						
Suspended sediment	$LOG(SEDQ)=0.0201(Q^{0.500})+0.405$	10	0.97	<0.001	34.9	1.01
Cadmium	$LOG(CDQ)=0.0832(Q^{0.333})-4.83$	10	.90	<.001	39.1	1.01
Copper	$CUQ=0.00000122(Q)^{1.26}$	10	.89	<.001	40.0	1.01
Iron	$LOG(FEQ)=0.123(Q^{0.333})-1.99$	10	.97	<.001	30.9	1.01
Lead	$LOG(PBQ)=0.0999(Q^{0.333})-3.92$	10	.92	<.001	43.5	1.01
Manganese	$LOG(MNQ)=0.0129(Q^{0.333})-1.63$	10	.94	<.001	32.6	1.01
Zinc	$ZNQ=0.000000708(Q)^{1.36}$	10	.86	<.001	50.5	1.02
Arsenic	$ASQ=0.0000310(Q)^{0.829}$	10	.90	<.001	24.5	1.00
Equations applied to and developed using data collected during the rising limb of the water year 2008 runoff period (March 9–May 21, 2008)						
Suspended sediment	$SEDQ=0.00000310(Q)^{2.19}$	8	0.94	<0.001	55.2	1.02
Cadmium	$CDQ=0.0000000120(Q)^{1.48}$	8	.89	<.001	54.1	1.02
Copper	$CUQ=0.00000531(Q)^{1.38}$	8	.88	<.001	52.1	1.02
Iron	$FEQ=0.000000679(Q)^{1.90}$	8	.94	<.001	48.6	1.02
Lead	$PBQ=0.000000490(Q)^{1.43}$	8	.88	<.001	53.4	1.02
Manganese	$MNQ=0.00000116(Q)^{1.58}$	8	.92	<.001	47.4	1.02
Zinc	$ZNQ=0.00000186(Q)^{1.53}$	8	.89	<.001	54.6	1.02
Arsenic	$ASQ=0.00000506(Q)^{1.14}$	8	.90	<.001	37.9	1.01

Table S3.2.   Regression equations for estimating suspended-sediment and unfiltered-recoverable trace-element discharge for Clark Fork at St. Regis, Mont. (station 12354500), water years 2006–09.—Continued

[Abbreviations: N, number of values; R^2, coefficient of determination; p-value, significance level; SE, standard error of estimate, in percent; RBCF, retransformation-bias-correction factor; SEDQ, suspended-sediment discharge, in tons per day; Q, streamflow, in cubic feet per second; CDQ, cadmium discharge, in tons per day; CUQ, copper discharge, in tons per day; FEQ, iron discharge, in tons per day; PBQ, lead discharge, in tons per day; MNQ, manganese discharge, in tons per day; ZNQ, zinc discharge, in tons per day; ASQ, arsenic discharge, in tons per day; LOG, base 10 logarithm. Symbol: <, less than]

Constituent	Equation	N	R^2	p-value	SE	RBCF
Equations applied to and developed using data collected during the rising limb of the water year 2009 runoff period (March 9–June 1, 2009)						
Suspended sediment	$SEDQ=0.000000120(Q)^{2.47}$	12	0.94	<0.001	56.3	1.02
Cadmium	$CDQ=0.00000000126(Q)^{1.55}$	12	.90	<.001	45.4	1.02
Copper	$CUQ=0.0000000386(Q)^{1.72}$	12	.88	<.001	56.2	1.02
Iron	$FEQ=0.0000000566(Q)^{2.09}$	12	.91	<.001	60.2	1.02
Lead	$PBQ=0.00000000195(Q)^{1.86}$	12	.85	<.001	71.3	1.03
Manganese	$MNQ=0.000000737(Q)^{1.57}$	12	.87	<.001	53.6	1.02
Zinc	$ZNQ=0.000000109(Q)^{1.66}$	12	.89	<.001	52.8	1.02
Arsenic	$ASQ=0.00000135(Q)^{1.20}$	12	.90	<.001	33.4	1.01
Equations applied to and developed using data collected during the falling limbs (and all other nonrising-limb periods) of water years 2008–09 (May 22, 2008–March 8, 2009; June 2–September 30, 2009)						
Suspended sediment	$SEDQ=0.000000000264(Q)^{3.01}$	8	0.97	<0.001	17.6	1.00
Cadmium	$CDQ=0.00000000000156(Q)^{2.17}$	8	.87	<.001	25.8	1.01
Copper	$CUQ=0.00000000184(Q)^{1.96}$	8	.92	<.001	18.4	1.00
Iron	$FEQ=0.000000000712(Q)^{2.46}$	8	.98	<.001	11.1	1.00
Lead	$PBQ=0.0000000000296(Q)^{2.20}$	8	.95	<.001	16.4	1.00
Manganese	$MNQ=0.000000000927(Q)^{2.17}$	8	.96	<.001	13.6	1.00
Zinc	$ZNQ=0.0000000000524(Q)^{2.36}$	8	.92	<.001	22.1	1.00
Arsenic	$ASQ=0.000000236(Q)^{1.36}$	8	.90	<.001	13.9	1.00

Table S3.3.   Regression equations for estimating suspended-sediment and unfiltered-recoverable trace-element discharge for Flathead River near Perma, Mont. (station 12388700), water years 2006–09.

[Abbreviations: N, number of values; R^2, coefficient of determination; p-value, significance level; SE, standard error of estimate, in percent; RBCF, retransformation-bias-correction factor; SEDQ, suspended-sediment discharge, in tons per day; Q, streamflow, in cubic feet per second; ND, not determined; CDQ, cadmium discharge, in tons per day; CUQ, copper discharge, in tons per day; LOG, base 10 logarithm; FEQ, iron discharge, in tons per day; PBQ, lead discharge, in tons per day; MNQ, manganese discharge, in tons per day; ZNQ, zinc discharge, in tons per day; ASQ, arsenic discharge, in tons per day. Symbol: <, less than]

Constituent	Equation	N	R^2	p-value	SE	RBCF
	Equations applied to and developed from data collected during the rising limbs of the water years 2006–07 and 2009 runoff periods (March 21–June 20, 2006; March 3–June 20, 2007; March 9–June 8, 2009)					
Suspended sediment	$SEDQ=0.00000534(Q)^{1.82}$	33	0.83	<0.001	49.0	1.02
Cadmium	ND	ND	ND	ND	ND	ND
Copper	$CUQ=0.0000000147(Q)^{1.46}$	32	.84	<.001	37.0	1.01
Iron	$LOG(FEQ)=0.073(Q^{0.333})-1.32$	33	.85	<.001	35.4	1.01
Lead	$PBQ=0.0000000212(Q)^{1.28}$	33	.77	<.001	41.0	1.01
Manganese	$MNQ=0.000000791(Q)^{1.31}$	33	.88	<.001	28.6	1.01
Zinc	$LOG(ZNQ)=0.00610(Q^{0.500})-2.32$	32	.40	<.001	69.3	1.04
Arsenic	$ASQ=0.000000704(Q)^{1.05}$	33	.98	<.001	8.6	1.00
	Equations applied to and developed using data collected during the rising limb of the water year 2008 runoff period (March 9–May 27, 2008)					
Suspended sediment	$SEDQ=0.000000026(Q)^{2.43}$	11	0.89	<0.001	50.9	1.02
Cadmium	ND	ND	ND	ND	ND	ND
Copper	$CUQ=0.000000000154(Q)^{2.01}$	11	.66	.002	101.1	1.07
Iron	$FEQ=0.0000000047(Q)^{2.16}$	11	.95	<.001	28.8	1.01
Lead	$PBQ=0.0000000000185(Q)^{2.05}$	11	.92	<.001	35.7	1.01
Manganese	$MNQ=0.0000000084(Q)^{1.82}$	11	.97	<.001	19.5	1.00
Zinc	$ZNQ=0.000000000096(Q)^{2.05}$	11	.96	<.001	23.7	1.00
Arsenic	$LOG(ASQ)=0.0629(Q^{0.333})-3.28$	11	.99	<.001	7.6	1.00
	Equations applied to and developed using data collected during the falling limbs (and all other nonrising-limb periods) of water years 2006–09 (October 1, 2005–March 20, 2006; June 21, 2006–March 2, 2007; June 21, 2007–March 8, 2008; May 28, 2008–March 8, 2009; June 9–September 30, 2009)					
Suspended sediment	$LOG(SEDQ)=0.103(Q^{0.333})-0.371$	10	0.97	<0.001	27.5	1.01
Cadmium	ND	ND	ND	ND	ND	ND
Copper	$CUQ=0.0000000876(Q)^{1.27}$	9	.89	<.001	32.9	1.01
Iron	$LOG(FEQ)=0.0915(Q^{0.333})-1.88$	10	.96	<.001	27.9	1.01
Lead	$PBQ=0.000000000137(Q)^{1.77}$	10	.94	<.001	33.6	1.01
Manganese	$LOG(MNQ)=0.0730(Q^{0.333})-2.52$	10	.95	<.001	24.4	1.00
Zinc	$ZNQ=0.000640(Q)^{0.0114}$	10	.96	<.001	24.2	1.00
Arsenic	$LOG(ASQ)=0.00620(Q^{0.500})-2.50$	10	.94	<.001	16.0	1.00